THEY CALLED US GIRLS

THEY CALLED US GIRLS

Stories of Female
Ambition from
Suffrage to Mad Men

Kathleen
Courtenay
Stone

CYNREN
CHESTER COUNTY,
PENNSYLVANIA

Published by Cynren Press
101 Lindenwood Drive, Suite 225
Malvern, PA 19355 USA
http://www.cynren.com/

First published 2022

Printed in the United States of America on acid-free paper

ISBN-13: 978-1-947976-24-5 (hbk)
ISBN-13: 978-1-947976-25-2 (ebk)

Library of Congress Control Number: 2021942058

For information about special discounts for bulk purchases, please contact Cynren Press Sales at (484) 875–3113 or sales.media@cynren.com

Cynren Press has no responsibility for the persistence or accuracy of URLs for external or third-party internet websites referred to in this publication and does not guarantee that any content on such websites is, or will remain, accurate or appropriate.

Every effort has been made to trace the ownership of copyrighted material. Information that will enable the publisher to rectify any error or omission in subsequent reprints will be welcome. In such cases, please contact the publisher at press@cynren.com.

Cover design by Emma Hall

For my sister and my mother

Contents

Illustrations

Acknowledgments

Writing a book is a long, solitary process. At least it was for me. I began working on what I called a "project" more than ten years ago, without knowing that the amorphous project would grow into this book. But it did, evolving from casual chats to interviews, from notes to chapters, from rough drafts to manuscript. Given the solitary nature of the research and writing in which I was engaged, I had the sense to embrace the wisdom of others. Thank you to all whose paths I crossed, particularly those mentioned here.

My deepest thanks go to the women who graciously shared their stories with me. Dahlov Ipcar, Muriel Petioni, Cordelia Hood, Martha Lepow, Mildred Dresselhaus, Frieda Garcia, and Rya Zobel, along with your families and colleagues—I could not have done it without you. Also, Charlie Ipcar, Bob Ipcar, Charles Woolfolk, Sarah Fisher, and Shoshi Cooper—you were invaluable sources of memories and photographs. Lauren Lepow,

I was saddened to hear of Martha's death just as the book went to press, but I thank you for telling me. Many other women also deviated from the paths others expected them to follow, and I wish I could have talked to all of them. The least I can do is say thank you for lighting the way for those of us who came after you.

Holly Monteith and the team at Cynren Press, particularly Cindy Durand, made a publishing home for me. It was the right match, and I am so glad we found each other. Emma Hall, thank you for the cover design.

It is my good fortune to be part of several wonderful communities of writers who are committed to their craft and happy to extend a hand of friendship. Biographers International, the Boston Biographers group, and two roundtable discussion groups—on women's biography and group biography—have provided me with colleagues and a wealth of expertise. Thank you, everyone.

The Bennington writing community is a source of endlessly creative and varied writing, and steady support. Particular thanks to Martha Wolfe and Laura Lipson for guiding me through early drafts. And to my friend Jean Hey, thank you for your boundless encouragement and wisdom, dispensed in countless cafés around Boston.

Kathy Weld, thank you for having the idea that I should read the manuscript aloud to you. That helped me hear where the writing had wandered off, and those afternoons were much more fun than reading to myself in front of the bathroom mirror.

My deep appreciation goes to editors Mary Carol Moore and Anne Horowitz. I met them at different stages of the book's development, and each offered just what the book needed at that time. If gaps or errors exist in what I have written, it is only because I did not listen to you carefully enough. Thank you to Justice Gabrielle Wolohojian for the introduction and to photographer Rick Salemi and attorney Jonathan Handler for suggesting pictures of Judge Zobel. And Jackie Anderson at Colortek of Boston—you are a wizard with all things photographic.

I am eternally grateful to my family for all things. My parents and sister remain with me in spirit. To my brother Larry, who shares my belief that childhood memories are worth plumbing for meaning, thank you for joining me in the endeavor and helping me remember more deeply. To my sister-in-law Patty, thank you for your suggestions and making your incredible network available to me. James, you once said to me, when I was experiencing an early-stage fit of uncertainty, "Mom, you can do it." I never forgot your words, and they sustained throughout. And to Andrew, thank you for everything. You are my true north.

Introduction

In my memory's eye, I see an eight-year-old girl sitting cross-legged on the living room floor, next to a bookshelf. It's Sunday afternoon, after the big dinner that follows church, and the house is peaceful. My father is reading, and my mother is paying bills at the kitchen table. For once, my little sister and brother are quiet. As my family fades into the background, I am alone, eyeing my father's books. Different sizes, variously colored, mostly hardback, thick and dry, there is little here to amuse me. Out of a combination of boredom and curiosity, I pull a few off the shelf.

My father has written his name on the flyleafs in neat, penciled script, sometimes with a date and location. Inside *The Divine Comedy,* it says "Bowdoin College, 1940." *The Thurber Carnival* reads "Okinawa, 1945." It's "Apley Hall, Cambridge, 1946" inside *A History of the United States Navy.* Inside the fattest book, *Black's Law Dictionary,* it says "Dwight Street, New Haven, 1948." Someday, I think, I will read books like these.

But this afternoon, I want something I can understand. A book with pictures would be nice. Scanning the spines, I recognize a cover of robin's-egg blue and gold letters. I've seen it before, and I know it has pictures. It's the Yale Law School yearbook, class of 1950.

I cradle the book on my lap and flip to my father's picture. With his posed smile, he looks young and anxious to please. I squirm a little to see him in this unfamiliar way. When I survey the rest of the class, I see more than a hundred men in jackets, ties, and trim haircuts, and maybe ten women.

I don't know any women lawyers. In our neighborhood, most women are like my mother—home taking care of kids—but I'm intrigued by the idea that some women, somewhere, are different. I want to know what makes a woman become a lawyer.

I linger over the pictures, squinting. Maybe if I concentrate enough, I will pull answers out of them. Some are pretty like my mother. Some wear a necklace; others don't. The ones with glasses look smart. This is an entirely superficial approach, I now realize, but on that day, I stare, hoping an answer will reveal itself. No matter how long I look, the women keep their secrets.

I am not always so serious. Most days, I play with kids in the neighborhood. We live in a suburb west of Boston, where out in the street, kids play ball, stepping aside when a car approaches before swarming behind to catch the sweet-smelling exhaust from leaded gas. When Hula-Hoops come on the scene, I am a champion hip swiveler. I watch a lot of television.

Leave It to Beaver is one of my favorite shows. I get the comedy—kids trying to outwit parents and parents sniffing out the truth. I also get the family dynamic, with June Cleaver at home and Ward at the office. Yet the Cleavers and my family are not entirely similar. Unlike June, my mother does not wear pearls in the kitchen, and my father is very hands-on with laundry and kitchen cleanup, whereas Ward is not. But other things about the show are intuitively familiar. I am a baby boomer, born near the end of the postwar boom. Our town is full of families like mine. All are white. The men commute into the city, and most of the women stay home. Only two women on our street have jobs outside the home; one is divorced, and the other has no children.

Finally, I give up. Staring at the yearbook pictures has gotten me nowhere. I have no clue why these women took a path different from my mother's, but I suspect some secret ingredient is at work, something I have not yet discovered. I close the yearbook and put it back on the shelf.

I will have to look elsewhere for answers, and I start with Dad. I plop down on the couch, he puts the newspaper aside, and I ask, Why weren't there more women in your law school class?

He doesn't act surprised, but he seldom does.

"That's just the way things were," he says.

"What does that mean—the way things were?"

"Tradition," he says. "It's not that women can't go to law school, they just tend not to. Most want to be home, taking care of their families."

There has to be more to it than this, I think. He's not saying how tradition came to be. Or why only women, but not men, want to be home.

Later I find my mother and try again.

"Why weren't there more women in Dad's law school class?"

"The war had a lot to do with it," she says. "We waited for the war to be over, to get married and start families. When it was over, that's what we did."

But something is missing. Mom worked at IBM before I was born. She has told me about traveling to customer offices and demonstrating the latest equipment. From the way she talks, I know she liked the job.

"What about IBM?" I ask. "Don't you miss it?"

"I love being a mother. To me, that's the most important thing."

The fifties and sixties of my childhood were more complex than *Leave It to Beaver*, but the show did capture some truths. Women were indeed discouraged from entering realms outside the home. The public-facing roles in government and business were filled by men, where they set policy, made money, and lived out their ambitions. I had no perspective on that when I was a child. All I saw was Mom at home and Dad going to the office. I knew nothing of the first wave of feminism, which had ended decades before I was born. The fact that I was growing up in a period that was quiet, from a feminist perspective, was entirely lost on me.

I had no inkling that I would eventually go to law school or that, when I did, second wave feminism would be cresting.[1]

Late in my own legal career, I found myself wondering about women of my mother's generation who had professional careers. Questions from when I was eight still lurked; I had only pushed them aside while I made my own career. After more than twenty years as a lawyer, I was back to wondering where women found their ambition, when almost every cultural message preached against it. Now, however, I knew that staring at pictures was not going to work. I would have to dig for answers.

To begin, I read books on women's history and got a sense of trends and statistics. I learned about the progress women made in the late nineteenth and early twentieth centuries, when they and their allies pushed boundaries across a variety of political and social fronts, advocating a new and broader role for women. Not only should women be permitted to vote, they said, but women should have access to robust education and be free to deploy their talents in the workplace.

In 1914, a meeting was held that its organizers billed as the "first feminist mass meeting." Actually, there were two meetings, both at Cooper Union in New York. At the first, speakers explained what feminism meant to them. The definitions ran the gamut, but the one that rang most true to women entering the professions came from George Middleton. He was a playwright whose oeuvre included *Back of the Ballot Box: A Woman Suffrage Farce in One Act,* a lighthearted take on feminism. Off the stage, he took the subject seriously. Feminism, he said, was an "educational ideal." Children should "be educated according to temperament and not according to maleness and femaleness. It asks that girls be educated for work and not for sex."[2] Three days later, at the second feminist mass meeting, his wife advised women to keep their surnames when they married, as she had done. Not Mrs. Middleton, she was Fola La Follette.[3]

Six years later, women achieved notable success when the Nineteenth Amendment to the Constitution was ratified. Also by 1920, at least one-third of the students who earned a bachelor's or master's degree were women, and women held about 15 percent of professional jobs. Today, those seem like small fractions, but they represented significant progress considering that, for much of the nineteenth century, most women who worked outside the home were engaged in agricultural, factory, or domestic work.[4]

Still, there was room for improvement. Progress was not distributed equally among racial and ethnic groups. A nonwhite woman was less likely to find work in a professional field than was her white counterpart. Also, staying home and forgoing an income was not an option for many, even if the dominant cultural message was that women should do just that.

Very few women of any race pursued either a doctorate or a first professional degree in medicine, law, or dentistry. Instead, they clustered in teaching and nursing, fields that were considered appropriate for women. Nevertheless, there was, in 1920, considerable optimism about the future. Women had voting rights, a respectable share of college degrees, and a toehold in the professional sector, all harbingers of progress.

As things turned out, the achievements of 1920 did not glide into a continuous upward trend. After suffrage, a split occurred among women's groups, unable to agree on shared goals. In education, women's achievement levels would fluctuate in the decades ahead, and sometimes decline.

One fact stands out from the rest, even in this story of halting, uneven progress. After 1920, women's share of professional jobs stopped growing; women were essentially stranded on a plateau. For a full half-century, their share of the professional world did not budge. Not until the 1970s did women resume making inroads into male-dominated professions. As Nancy Cott, a noted historian, wrote, "one can generalize to the extent of saying that the high point in women's share of professional employment (and attainment of advanced degrees) overall occurred by the late 1920s and was followed by stasis and/or decline not reversed to any extent until the 1960s and 1970s."[5]

This stagnant period is exactly the time when the women about whom I was curious started their careers. How did they find the ambition, confidence, sense of self—whatever it was—to have a professional career when the culture said not to, and most of their contemporaries agreed? To find out, I would have to talk to women themselves.

As I began to search for women to interview, my first criterion was date of birth. I needed to find women who were, roughly speaking, contemporaries of my mother, who was born in 1922. Also, I wanted to interview "professionals," but there is no fixed definition of that word. *Professional* means one thing in common speech, or even multiple things, and something else again in Census Bureau classifications. Even the census definition evolves over time.[6] Furthermore, some professional fields were so thoroughly populated by women that they had effectively become "women's" jobs. I was determined to interview women who had veered into less familiar terrain.[7]

By the time I set out to find them, women who met my criteria were in their eighties and nineties. Some who would have given a splendid interview a decade earlier were not available. Not everyone of that age wants to be, or can be, interviewed. The range of possibilities narrowed further when I took ethnic and socioeconomic diversity into account. Because of legal, societal, and cultural barriers, few Black, Latina, or Asian women had worked in male-dominated professions in that era. On top of that, some women said no to my interview request or simply did not respond. With each criterion and hurdle, the group of possible interview subjects narrowed.

Another decision I had to make was whether to seek women who were famous. Every woman I interviewed was well regarded in her field, and some received extraordinary professional honors, but none is famous in a household-name kind of way. That was intentional. Once a name is up in lights, the fame can feed on itself. A truer way to figure out what accounted for professional ambition was to look at women who succeeded without the boost of fame. Sometimes a friend or colleague offered to introduce me to someone with a high profile, but I politely declined. I did not want one famous woman to skew the book. I feared all eyes would be on her and not on the whole.

To find women to interview, I surveyed the internet, combed through lists, contacted schools and professional associations, and talked to my network. Friends and colleagues were invariably helpful with suggestions.

It probably goes without saying that I was doing this on an infinitesimally small scale without research team or budget, guided by questions I had had since I was young, now updated and expanded by maturity and experience. Not intended as a quantitative study, it was qualitative research, which I hoped would be equally enlightening.

The seven portraits that follow were selected from more than a dozen interviews. They reflect a diversity of job, race, ethnicity, and socioeconomic origin. They are arranged in a sequence to illustrate how, even during the fifty years when women were stuck, statistically speaking, opportunities evolved, often in response to historic events and political mood.

The writer Candice Millard describes biography as a bridge that runs between the reader and the person whose life is on the page. "It's hard to read about someone else's life without seeing something of oneself," she said in her keynote speech at a biography conference I attended. "We are connected in some fundamental way."[8]

Interviewing women for the book, I knew she was right. I did see something of myself in the life stories I was hearing. Later, when I wrote, I found myself inhabiting two perspectives: the grown women who conducted the interviews and the naive eight-year-old girl who wondered about women in the first place. Both are in the chapters that follow.

1

The First Wave Recedes
Dahlov Zorach Ipcar, Artist
(b. 1917)

Dahlov Ipcar was ninety-six when we met. I had known her name for decades, ever since overhearing my parents read her picture book *Lobsterman* to my little brother. The story line hooked me. It's about a boy named Larry who lives in Maine and spends a day lobstering with his father. In the weeks leading up to this particular day, they paint buoys, repair traps, sand and paint the boat. Out on the water, they set traps, including one just for Larry. When they return the next day to haul traps, they find three lobsters caught in Larry's, just enough for dinner. At home, Larry's mother waits, a big pot of steaming water at the ready. The boy is so pleased with the catch that he vows to become a lobsterman.

The story line sounds saccharine now, but then, it did not seem so. The father working away from the house, the mother waiting to cook dinner—this was familiar. So was the idea of a child being intrigued by the father's work. Also, the book seemed to have a magical, if improbable, connection to my family—Larry was my brother's and my father's name; my family spent time in Maine in the summer; we had a ramshackle cottage on the beach, not far from where my grandparents lived. No one in my family lobstered for a living, but Dahlov's rendering of wooden traps, hand-painted buoys, and seagulls coasting overhead captured the landscape I knew. The visual clarity and emotional content of her images remained with me into adulthood, so much so that when I had my own son, I read the book to him.

Years later, when I was working on this book, I came across a Maine lifestyle magazine with an article about Dahlov. Eureka! She fit my age criterion, and she was an artist, an unusual career for her generation. I found her address on the internet and wrote a letter, and within the week, she called to invite me to her house. Her voice on the phone was deep and steady, only a little crinkly at the edges.

I drove to Bath, Maine, three hours from my home in Boston, then south on the Georgetown peninsula, watching for a shed covered with lobster pots—my landmark. There I turned into a long driveway and wound past massive rhododendrons and deep green ferns before coming to a clearing with a weathered barn, other small outbuildings, and the white, shingle-clad house where Dahlov waited at the front door. She led me inside, leaning on a walker that she had outfitted with cloth pockets stuffed with a sweater, a bottle of water, two plastic cups, and a cell phone—everything she might need for our afternoon together.

As we walked to her studio on the back side of the house, we passed through rooms where walls were gently out of plumb and wide floorboards, under their polished sheen, showed wear. She had been in this house nearly eighty years, first with her husband and two sons, and now alone. Several times on our walk to the studio, she paused to remark on artwork. Both her parents, Marguerite Thompson Zorach and William Zorach, were artists, noted members of the early modernist movement. In the living room, she pointed out several of her mother's paintings, including portraits of herself as a young girl. Her father was best known as a sculptor, and studies for his larger works, blocky yet curvy figures, were arranged on shelves. We ducked into a bedroom, where Dahlov showed me her mother's hooked rug with a sinuous figure of a female nude.

When we reached the studio door, I saw a triptych, positioned like a folding screen. It was an early work of Dahlov's, painted when she was eighteen, of rural Maine in the dead of winter.

ILLUS. 1.1 Dahlov Ipcar in her studio, 2011. Photograph courtesy of Bob Ipcar.

Once inside the studio, I was surrounded by a profusion of colorful canvases with fanciful depictions of animals.

Dahlov had grown up thoroughly immersed in early modern art, and she incorporated some of its innovations into her own work. In her hands, cubism was incorporated into brightly colored pictures of zebras, horses, and cows, an unorthodox approach that made me wonder what else was novel about her approach to art and career.

As a girl, Dahlov lived in Greenwich Village, only a few blocks from where feminist mass meetings were held shortly before she was born. It was a neighborhood crowded with various nationalities and ethnicities. Many people were artists and political outsiders, prone to challenging anything that was traditional and expected. A bohemian spirit filled the streets.

"We lived on West Tenth Street, across from the women's prison," Dahlov remembered. "It was an amazing Gothic structure. Underneath the jail was the Jefferson Market. There were bail bond lawyers up and down the street. Everybody thought it was a dreadful neighborhood, but nothing bad ever happened to me there."

Inside the family's apartment, her parents painted the floors red and the walls lemon yellow. To one wall, they added a life-sized tableau of Adam and Eve, the snake slithering down the tree. Their Eve was neither subservient to Adam nor his corrupter; she was his partner in the Garden of Eden, partaking equally in its delights and dangers, a reflection of Marguerite's and William's goals for their own lives.

They met as art students in Paris in the early 1900s, when that city was the center of avant-garde art. Form, color, spatial relationships, and subject matter—all were ripe for experimentation. They plunged into the scene, and Marguerite was an occasional visitor to the home of Gertrude and Leo Stein, where some of the city's most noted artists came together. Endlessly, the young couple talked about art and a future in which women and men would be treated equally as artists.

By 1912, they were back in New York and married, readying work to exhibit in the Armory Show, the 1913 landmark exhibition of modern art. The show was controversial, even outrageous, to those who were getting their first look at contemporary art, but that was exactly where Marguerite and William wanted their work to be seen. When the doors to the National Guard armory on Lexington Avenue opened to the public, their work hung alongside that of artists whose paintings the couple had admired in Paris—Georges Braque, Paul Cézanne, Marcel Duchamp, Paul Gaugin, Henri Matisse, Claude Monet, Pablo Picasso, Pierre-Auguste Renoir, Vincent van Gogh. A year later, the couple had their first child, a boy named Tessim, followed by Dahlov in 1917.

The apartment they had painted so colorfully was also their studio and impromptu viewing space. They invited other artists and friends to see their work and socialize, for fun and as part of the slow process of building a reputation and selling art. Many evenings were filled with people coming, going, and conversing about art. Dahlov remembered the pleasant hubbub. "Our house was very exciting. Interesting people came by all the time—Wallace Stevens, Marianne Moore, William Carlos Williams, Marsden Hartley. We had no money, but there was a lot of art, color, and conversation, and a wonderful spirit."

I conjure the apartment as it might have looked on an afternoon. William is working on a sculpture, wood shavings scattered on the floor. Marguerite is in another room, eyeing a painting and thinking about the color she is about to add. Ella, the woman who takes care of the children, has the day off, and the children are underfoot. "Let's build a tower," Tessim says, "the tallest one ever," and Dahlov agrees. They pull all their wooden blocks into the living room and stack them into an intricately balanced tower. While the children are busy, Marguerite hurries to try out her color. Soon she will be in the kitchen cooking dinner. Garlic, ginger, turmeric, cumin—spices she discovered on a trip during her Paris sojourn—will go into the curry. Then there will be a knock on the door, and an artist friend will arrive. If other evenings are a guide, they will talk until late at night about art. The children's block tower will eventually topple, but not before Marguerite captures it in a portrait of her four-year-old daughter which, ninety-some years later, Dahlov will point out to me as we walk through her living room.

One particularly happy aspect of Dahlov's young life was Ella Madison. Ella was an actor and singer who took the job of caring for the Zorach children when she was between gigs and brought unusual creativity to the job. She played with the children, sang songs, and talked to them about right and wrong. Dahlov remembered her as "a surrogate mother, a marvelous woman. She was a professional singer and sang Negro spirituals. I grew up on those." According to one story, she even staged scenes in Washington Square Park, where passersby would see Tessim insult her and then watch her dramatic reaction. Given that she was Black and he was white, this really would have gotten attention.[1]

Ella worked for the family for ten years, until she landed a part in the play *Porgy*, which was being produced by the Theatre Guild in New York with an almost entirely African American

ILLUS. 1.2   Marguerite Zorach, *Block Castle,* 1921. Oil on canvas,
18 × 15 inches. Private collection.

cast. The director's daughter was in school with Dahlov, which
led William to make an introduction. Ella was so impressive at
the audition that she was hired on the spot. *Porgy* later evolved
into the libretto for the opera *Porgy and Bess,* but during its initial
run, Ella, then seventy-three years old, performed nightly on
Broadway. When the cast headed overseas, she joined the others
for what was her tenth tour of Europe.[2]

Ella was the reason Marguerite was able to work as an artist.
As much as Marguerite and William shared an ideal of gender

equality, they lived, as we all do, in their own time. In theirs, women were expected to sew and cook, unless they were wealthy enough to have a maid. Even an artist did not escape these expectations, and art inspired Marguerite in her domestic work. She made most of the family's clothing, usually of her own design, and she cooked, often recipes imported from abroad. If, on top of that, she had spent most of her days with the children, she would have had no time at all for art. Though it was a financial stretch to hire Ella for childcare, it was necessary if Marguerite were to realize her ambitions as an artist.

William helped with housework, but it was not his primary responsibility. As he wrote in his autobiography, Marguerite "was frustrated at not having any uninterrupted time for painting, and uninterrupted time was a necessity for the kind of painting she did in oil. It was not something she could turn off and on; it was something she built up in a creative conception and had to see through. To be distracted or torn away at a crucial moment was very destructive to her. There was no uninterrupted time with caring for two small children, cooking, and running a house; and running a house came hard for her. I helped, but it didn't come easy to me either."[3]

In other ways, Marguerite deviated wildly from expectations of the era. Art was an unusual profession for women. According to the 1930 census, only twenty-one thousand women throughout the country were artists, and many of them also taught in public schools. Domestic work was far more common: almost four hundred times more women were domestics than were artists.[4]

As a young girl, Dahlov probably did not appreciate just how unconventional her mother was. What she did grasp, though, was the sense that everything was possible. "My mother could do anything," she said. "I assumed a woman could be an artist and have a husband and children too." Equally indelible was her mother's mark as an artist. As Dahlov said, "my parents were real innovators in their day, very modern. And my mother was the more innovative of the two."

William also had a big impact on his daughter. Chiseling wood sculptures or sketching in the living room, he could not help but be in the thick of family life. He also made a point of spending time alone with Dahlov. Some days, they visited the animals at the Central Park Zoo. Other times, they looked at art around the city. "He took me around to art museums and shows and artists' studios, when I wasn't in school. Part of his work was to see what was going on. He would go to the Metropolitan, for instance, and visit certain things. There was one Egyptian mouse he would go and study. There was one Greek warrior. One thing in each department."

His way of studying art became a blueprint for Dahlov. "He said it was to keep himself on the right track, and I feel that way too. I go look at things I admire." It also sparked her interest in other civilizations. "One of the first things I was interested in was cave art. My parents had a book about cave art, which nobody else had in those days."

Even more important was her father's belief that she was capable of serious work. Early on in the writing of this book, I approached a woman, then in her eighties, for an interview. She was a psychoanalyst who turned me down for the very good reason that she did not want patients reading about her personal life. During our phone conversation, she asked what themes were emerging from my interviews and was not surprised to hear that many women had strong relationships with their fathers. Nor was I, but her knowledge was considerably deeper than a layperson's.

She had studied a concept she called "endeavor excitement" and sent me a book chapter she had written on the subject. Part of a young girl's normal development, she wrote, is to individuate from her mother. In that process, a girl normally turns her attention to her father. When her father reciprocates and engages his daughter in projects, even those that are playful, he signals that her capabilities are not gender linked or limited. A girl lucky to have such a father, as Dahlov was, is more likely to emerge into adulthood with a vitality for work.[5]

In 1971, Linda Nochlin, the art historian, wrote a landmark essay titled "Why Have There Been No Great Women Artists?" Her title, deliberately provocative, referred to a question often asked by two camps: those who despaired of seeing women flourish, and those who doubted they ever could. The essay made the point that for centuries, men had decided what was great, defining the terms for success and training younger men. What would have happened, Nochlin mused, if Picasso had been born a girl? "Would Señor Ruiz have paid as much attention or stimulated as much ambition for achievement in a little Pablita?" Maybe Señor Ruiz would have ignored a daughter with artistic talent, but William did not ignore Dahlov. All the afternoons they spent together in studios and museums, on top of her genuine interest in the subject, stimulated a belief that she could do this work.[6]

Despite being artists, Dahlov's parents did not formally instruct her. "They showed me how to use a brush and some paints, and then left me alone. I never went to art school or had lessons." But at school, she was free to pursue her passion. She and Tessim attended the City and Country School, which had recently opened in the Village. Under its progressive approach, children were encouraged to follow their interests, which, for Dahlov, was art. "We used to all paint on the floor together," she remembered. "As we grew older, I begged the other kids to keep painting, but they didn't. I have a theory that kids stop painting because they start trying to please other people and that takes the joy out of it."

Dahlov also was a keen observer of the New York art scene. "We went to parties when I was growing up. My mother would sit in the corner and my father would circulate around. Also, we had friends where the women were artists along with their husbands. Most of the women artists took a back seat to their husbands. My mother did to a certain extent with my father. She just didn't promote herself, but he did. He was pretty good at that."

The larger culture only amplified the disparity between men and women artists. In 1916, the Zorachs were two of seventeen artists included in the Forum Exhibition of Modern American Painters, but, as Jessica Nicoll wrote in an essay for the Portland Museum of Art, Marguerite was the only woman. She was also the only one not to have an artist's statement or an artwork included in the catalog. Nicoll also noted that when *Vanity Fair* magazine ran an article in 1923 on the best painters in America, the caption below a photograph of William read, "There are two Zorachs. This one is William. The other is Marguerite. Both are talented and astonishingly prolific masters in many mediums." Ten years after exhibiting in the Armory Show, Marguerite had become the invisible "other" Zorach.[7]

Galleries also treated women as secondary. Take, for instance, painter Rebecca Salsbury, who was married to photographer Paul Strand, or Helen Torr, Arthur Dove's wife (both painters). Their husbands were regulars at galleries run by Alfred Stieglitz, then the most influential arbiter of artistic taste in New York, but the women found it difficult to make an independent mark. When Stieglitz gave Torr a show in 1933, *ArtNews* dismissed her work as derivative:

> [Stieglitz's gallery is] showing a group of paintings by Helen Torr (who is, in private life, Mrs. [Arthur] Dove), a procedure similar to that of the Strand exhibition, when one room is given over to paintings by Mrs. Strand. Mrs. Dove alternates between abstract and naturalistic effects, and as often as not pays her husband the sincere compliment of following in his footsteps.[8]

It is true that Torr and Dove shared artistic concerns, as did the Zorachs. But studying Torr's work at a recent exhibition, I found it impossible to say whether Dove influenced Torr or the converse.[9]

One woman who did get attention was Georgia O'Keefe. As Stieglitz's lover, then his wife, she had access to gallery shows that others did not. When he exhibited nude photos of her, the art world definitely talked. When he promoted a sexual interpretation of her flower paintings, the public was enthralled. In a letter to a friend, he expressed his view that women were nonintellectual beings, ruled by gender-specific emotion: "Woman feels the World differently than Man feels it. . . . The Woman receives the World through her Womb. That is the seat of her deepest feeling. Mind comes second."[10] Given that Stieglitz was so prominent in the art world, it is hardly surprising that critics and gallery owners, almost all of them men, found it difficult to take women artists seriously.

Dahlov was old enough to understand her mother's view of the art world. She was a teenager when Marguerite, then president of the New York Society of Women Artists, gave a newspaper interview in which she spoke about gallery representation: "If a woman approaches a dealer for an exhibit," she told the *Christian Science Monitor,* he often refuses. . . . Dealers take men artists under their wing, promote them, encourage them, push them as good business possibilities, but they usually refuse to take women artists seriously. Women artists are accused, both by the public and dealers, as having only a superficial interest in their art that does not last beyond love or marriage.[11]

For Marguerite, it was laughable to think her interest was only transitory. Art was her life's work, as it was for Dahlov, who painted well into her nineties.

Dahlov breathed in so much of the art world that, by the time she was a teenager, she considered whether it was the place for her. Art called to her, but so did animals. Pets, in multiples, were always part of the household. One of the paintings I saw in Dahlov's living room was Marguerite's portrait of her at age thirteen. She is holding a cat, a stray that became a beloved pet. More significant, though, is Dahlov's facial expression—astute and contemplative, parsing the world around her.

When she was twenty-two, Dahlov looked back at herself at the age she was in the portrait. The occasion was the Museum of Modern Art's exhibition of her childhood art, a show her father helped arrange. For the press release, Dahlov wrote,

> At the age of thirteen, I had a real renaissance. I began to be interested in people. As I became interested in the world around me, in political and social events and questions, etc., I suddenly realized—I don't know how—that realism was not important and that the beauty and feeling of the whole picture was what mattered.[12]

Part of this teenaged renaissance was her growing confidence about people, not only about art. When she began to describe her husband, her face lit up. "I met Adolph when I was fourteen and he was twenty-seven."

Her family had always spent summers outside the city, first in houses lent by friends, then in their own place, next to the house where Dahlov and I were talking. The property came with a well, trees for firewood, land for a garden, and space to build a privy—also a neighbor, whose brother arrived one summer

ILLUS. 1.3 Marguerite Zorach, *Dahlov and Tooky*, 1930. Oil on canvas, 42 × 26 inches. Private collection.

to help with farmwork. "Adolph was working in New York as an accountant, which he didn't like, and he came up for the summer. I was never interested in his sisters, but I found him interesting. He was very witty and fun. We did all kinds of things together."

Such as? "Once I told my brother we were going up into the woods to look for salamanders. He didn't believe me. He followed us, but then came back and said, 'My God, they really were up there looking for salamanders.'"

Dahlov left for Oberlin College in Ohio, where her first year was difficult. The art classes were old-fashioned and stultifying, nothing like the art world in which she had grown up. She thought about majoring in biology, given her love of animals, but worried she might lose her scholarship if she failed to master the academics. "Adolph came to visit me at Oberlin. I was bemoaning the fact that I didn't know what I wanted to do with my life. He thought I was joking—it was clear to him I would be an artist."

You know how the air crackles around two people who are falling in love? They think they can hide their feelings, but they inevitably send out silent signals that electrify the air. It must have been that way between Dahlov and Adolph. Marguerite felt the crackling air and started to set Adolph straight. "My mother thought he was in love with her," Dahlov told me. "She explained why a romance between them wouldn't work, but he said, oh no, I'm in love with your daughter. It was very embarrassing. As for me, I didn't give him an answer. I thought of marriage as something permanent, which it isn't nowadays. I didn't want to say no, and I didn't want to say yes, so we sort of left it at that." But she did decide not to return to Oberlin for her sophomore year. Instead, she would leave college, be an artist, and marry Adolph.

"My mother was supportive, but my father, on the other hand, was desperate. He didn't believe Adolph was the right man for me because he was not an artist. My father offered to send me to Paris. He thought I would fall in love with a Frenchman, and that would be all right with him."

William's disapproval of Adolph was highly ironic: he had once been the disfavored suitor himself. Before Marguerite went to Paris, her well-off family expected her to attend Stanford University, a plan she nixed when her aunt invited her to Paris. When she met William, she knew the relationship had to be kept secret: the poor young man would not be acceptable to her family. As Dahlov explained, "my father's family left Lithuania because of pogroms. My grandfather was a peddler, with nine children and no money." The family settled in Cleveland, Ohio, where William attended school through eighth grade, before he got a job in a lithograph shop to help support the family. Eventually, he went to art school in New York, then traveled to Paris.

When Marguerite's aunt figured out what was going on, she took her niece on a long tour of the Middle East and Asia, hoping the romance would fade away, but it didn't. Marguerite went to visit her parents in California, decided that was no longer the place for her, and boarded a train for New York. William met her at the station, and they were married the next day. But twenty-some years later, he was the protective father. An accountant was simply not suitable. That, more than the age gap, seemed to be the sticking point. Yet Dahlov, like her mother, had her own ideas and intended to act on them. "I knew I didn't want to marry an artist because I didn't want to become his model," she said.

Dahlov's not wanting to be a model seemed simple at first blush. She and Tessim often posed for their parents, too many times to count. Her parents put family at the center of their art. William even wrote in his autobiography, "I realized my art through them." When I reread the transcript of my interview with Dahlov, though, her words took on a different shade of meaning. Growing up around many two-artist couples, she had seen women take a back seat to their husbands, and she did not want that for herself. If she married Adolph, she would be the *only* artist, not the *other* artist, in the family.

For his part, William came to realize he was wrong about Adolph. He even made fun of himself. As he wrote, "I had liked my son-in-law before I found out he was going to marry my daughter."[13]

Getting married during the Great Depression was counter to trend. The high unemployment rate meant marriage rates dropped sharply. But Dahlov and Adolph were not swayed by what others were doing. Even with no end in sight to the economic distress, they married, gave up their jobs, and moved to Maine. With little in the way of a year-round art community, Dahlov knew she would be pioneering mostly on her own.[14]

ILLUS. 1.4   Dahlov Ipcar, *Winter in Maine,* 1935. Oil on board, 72 × 104 inches. Reproduced with permission of the artist.

Before they moved, Dahlov taught at a small school in Midtown Manhattan. When Adolph took a job there too, the school stopped paying her. A married woman, she was supposed to rely on her husband's income, not take a job that a more deserving man might need. This view was common before the Depression and became only more entrenched when men lost their jobs. But when Dahlov talked about their move, it was clear that they were pulled to Maine, more than pushed away by New York.[15]

"I always loved coming up to Maine at Christmastime with my family," she said, "and I thought Adolph and I would spend one winter and see what it was like. Of course, it was the Depression, and we gave up the jobs we had teaching, and it wasn't easy to get another job at a distance. When we finally did get a good job offer, we were settled in Maine. I had just had a baby, our first son, and we had just increased a herd of cows and bought a big flock of pigeons. We just didn't want to leave, so we stayed here and farmed. And I kept on painting."

Thinking about their move, it occurred to me that the triptych I had seen when we entered the studio was evidence of Dahlov's feelings. The rural winter scene she had painted was romantic, even mythic. Men dressed in overalls and boots wielded an axe and a handsaw. Other men field-dressed a deer, its antlers spread over the snow. A couple in a horse-drawn sleigh lingered to watch cows at the edge of a pond. She painted it when she and Adolph were in the throes of deciding whether to leave New York, and it made plain her joyous expectations for life ahead.

In Maine, they grew their own vegetables, and Adolph delivered their cows' milk to neighbors in a horse-drawn cart. "It was quite a challenge," she remembered, "but we did it all. Adolph learned to shoe a horse with an agricultural bulletin in one hand and a hammer in the other. We read farm books, antique books about farming. We felt romantic about it." A second son followed a few years after the first. And Dahlov painted her life—the farm animals, the Maine existence, the ordinary sights she loved.

A persistent question for women is how they combine their work with family life. When Dahlov was young, her mother's answer was to employ Ella Madison, but Dahlov worked things out differently. "People can't understand how you could farm and have children and still have time for your art. If you get up at five o'clock in the morning, you get an awful lot done. Adolph would get up and milk the cows. I would get the kids up and make breakfast, but I would also clean the house before breakfast. And then, after the kids went off to school, I had a lot of time to paint, especially in the winter. The only time I didn't paint was in the middle of the summer when we were haying, which was always a big deal because we did it the old-fashioned way with pitchforks and rakes and horses. Sometimes I spent four hours a day in the garden, just weeding. But you are young and you have energy."

As she had seen her parents at work, her boys saw Adolph and her at theirs. "The nice thing about a farm is that you are right there all the time and your kids see what you are doing. They see the work you do."

To advance her career, Dahlov submitted pictures to juried shows around the country and competed for government commissions. Under a New Deal program funded by the Treasury Section of Fine Arts, she painted murals for two post offices, in LaFollette, Tennessee, and Yukon, Oklahoma. The payments, $600 for each, were a big boost to the family's income.

Life on the farm did not change much, even when the war began in 1941. Adolph was too old to be drafted, and they continued farming and milking. "We really didn't have the news the way you do now. We had a certain amount of radio news and a certain amount of movie news, but not all this detail of all the things that were going on."

Even without an incessant news cycle, Dahlov knew that the art world was changing. Abstract expressionism was the new thing, and that's what collectors wanted. Her father encouraged her to maintain connections in New York, but she was not interested. "They just threw out everything that I liked and went in for abstract expressionism. I just didn't warm up to that kind of art. I liked all the variety."

The shift in collectors' tasks threatened to leave her and her art behind, but she made it a catalyst for a new round of soul searching. "The change made me stop and think what kind of art I wanted to do. I thought back to all the art I liked and decided I really wanted to do animals and I really wanted to do them my own way. I liked color and I liked to create my own thing. It wasn't what other people were doing, but it was what I wanted to do."

As we talked, an unfinished canvas sat on the easel in front of us with a brood of yellow-brown hens, their bodies in segments. The fragmented, feathered bodies seemed to pulse, alternating with slices of a yellow cubist background. It was not realistic, but not entirely abstract either. It was very much Dahlov's own thing.

Knowing what she wanted to paint was important, but that didn't make the work saleable. Making money was never Dahlov's primary goal. An artist is a "noneconomic" person, she said, who is happy as long as there is enough money for shelter, food, and art supplies. But some income would be welcome, because farming did not produce much. When a former teacher told Dahlov that Margaret Wise Brown needed an illustrator for her new book, she decided to give it a try. Brown had already published *The Runaway Bunny,* and for her new book, *The Little Fisherman,* it made sense to use an artist from the coast of Maine.

Dahlov prepared for the job by studying children's literature, starting with *Alice in Wonderland.* "John Tenniel's vision was entirely different from Lewis Carroll's," she explained. "Carroll wanted to get a model for him, but Tenniel said, 'I don't need a model any more than you need a multiplication table.' Yet his figures are perfect. The drapery, the hands, the gestures, the movements—they are just so natural. I'm not good with people. I can do animals easily, but I can't do people the way he did them. Also, I think Ernest Shepard's illustrations from *The Wind in the Willows* are just perfect."

When *The Little Fisherman* was published in 1945, it was another turning point for Dahlov. "I learned about writing from studying Margaret Wise Brown's book. At first, I thought there is nothing to this, and then I realized how important all the writing and the words and the rhythm were."

Two years later, Dahlov came out with her own children's book, *Animal Hide and Seek,* the first of thirty she would write and illustrate over her career. Her titles often referred to animals—*Brown Cow Farm, Bright Barnyard, Wild and Tame Animals, Deep Sea Farm,* and so on. Children's literature was a career pivot for her, even though her mother discouraged it. "My mother said never get involved with commercial art—it will just milk your brain dry. But that didn't apply to children's books. If anything, they inspired me to do a lot more things in art than I would have done." Her bold colors and clean lines worked well in children's books and were the very elements that first caught my attention in *Lobsterman.*

Lobsterman is more nuanced than it first appears. Dahlov herself had grown up in an unconventional family, where both parents influenced her career, and this brings me to a personal observation. When I was young and thinking about my future, I assumed I would have a paid job as my father did. I did not assume I would be a stay-at-home mother, although, in truth, I did not think much about my future as a mother. When the Larry character in the book decides to become a lobsterman like his father, I did not interpret that to mean that a child should follow in the footsteps of the same-gender parent. It made perfect sense to me to want to emulate the parent whose work seemed intriguing.

In 2001, when Dahlov was eighty-four, the Portland Museum of Art mounted an exhibition of her paintings, *Dahlov Ipcar: Seven Decades of Creativity,* shown together with her parents' work. "It was a big show with my mother and father's work

ILLUS. 1.5 Dahlov Ipcar, *Boy in Window*, 1962. From *Lobsterman*, written and illustrated by Dahlov Ipcar (Camden, Maine: Down East Books, 1962), pp. 1–2. Reprinted with permission of the author.

downstairs and my work on the whole second floor. I had two big galleries and two side galleries that I filled up with art. And all these people came—they had more people at my show than had ever come to any of their shows before. I was flabbergasted. I thought to have a following you had to be a teacher or in some kind of arts colony. I never was."

Her parents had caught the eye of wealthy collectors. Dahlov, in Maine, had not. "I didn't have patrons like they did. I had very few patrons. What happened was that my children's books raised whole generations to appreciate my art." The huge turnout at the museum validated decisions she had made years earlier—to live outside the mainstream art world, to paint her own vision, to make books for children. She did not strike me as someone who needed much external validation, but anyone would like to know that others have paid attention and liked what they have seen. The show, held only two years before Adolph's death at age ninety-eight, must have been a bittersweet capstone to their life in Maine. Dahlov would spend the next sixteen years alone, until she died at the age of ninety-nine.

I was curious whether Dahlov thought the art world had opened up to women in the years since she began working. I prodded her to talk about the issue. She told me about being on a panel with a male sculptor to judge student artwork. "There were two young artists in the running for the scholarship," she remembered. "One was a boy, and one was a girl. He was holding out for the boy because, he thought, the boy was more likely to go on and do something. I said, 'You mean the girl is just going to get married and be a housewife? You really are a male chauvinist!'" She laughed. "That was the first time I had used such language. It was right after Betty Friedan's book [*The Feminine Mystique*] came out in 1963."

The man's assumption was something she had known all her life. It is the same thing with which Marguerite had taken issue when she'd spoken to the newspaper—that art was simply a lark for women as they waited to get married. Though both Marguerite and Dahlov had refuted that idea by their own actions, I doubt Dahlov would have brought it up if I had not pressed her. She was such a positive person that even remembering she had used the word *chauvinist* made her laugh.

Her outlook was underscored by a dream she described to me toward the end of our afternoon. "Just recently," she said, "I had a dream where I had to go down to the barn. I guess Adolph must have been sick and I had to take care of the cows and milk them. I started down the hill. There was deep snow, and I had two pails of hot water. When I woke up, I understood what Adolph went through every day. He went down there with two pails of hot water and came back with two pails of milk, up that hill with ice and snow. It was hard. But we wanted this life."

Intermezzo

Like a Little Puppy

Dahlov Ipcar's earliest connection to her parents' line of work, which eventually became her own, was sensory. The art they produced and the act of making it, complete with wood shavings and palettes loaded with paint, were all around her. Before she was old enough to understand intellectually what they did, she experienced the sights, sounds, and smells of art making.

Not so for me. Yes, I smelled my mother's cooking, but my father's work was away in an office, invisible and silent. Had it been in front of me, I still could not have grasped it. A lawyer at the Federal Reserve Bank in Boston, my father dealt with banking regulations and monetary policy. Neither subject had sensory appeal. When he explained money's flow through the economy and the regulations that kept it safe and efficient, I was lost.

Later, when people asked me why I went to law school, I gave a pat answer: my father was a lawyer. I would say it offhandedly, as though everyone intuitively understood that his choice of work influenced mine. More recently, though, having spent many hours speaking with other women and picking through the arcs of their lives to assess what bits of information are most significant, I have come to realize that no one thing explains it all. When I turn the magnifying glass from their lives to my own, myriad memories of small things come into focus.

When I was young, I was with my mother all day. She gave me all the attention any child could want. We did errands and colored pictures. She read stories and taught me the alphabet. But around age two, according to what she later told me, I began to sit at the window and wait for my father to come home. I was not so interested in the one who was there; I wanted the one who was absent. When he did come home, my father remembered it this way: "You followed me around like a little puppy dog. I couldn't shake you."

When he did chores, he let me watch. I was more hindrance than help, but he let me be with him, and we talked. When I was older, we rode bikes around our town, bodysurfed at the beach, skated on frozen ponds, raked leaves, washed storm windows, and, every night, did the dishes.

Once a year, my mother would drive us kids into Boston to visit him at the office. We always started with a tour, and certain details have stayed with me. There was the sight of millions of dollars being sorted in the bank's counting room. The supervisor would have us guess the number of dollars going through the machines, and no matter how astronomical the number we came up with, it was too low. The boardroom walls were covered in moss green corduroy, a nubby texture I rubbed with my fingers. The lobby featured murals by N. C. Wyeth of George Washington and Abraham Lincoln conferring with their treasury secretaries. These details did not explain what my father actually did, but they gave me an idea of the context in which he worked.

More important, though, were the hours my father spent taking me seriously. The conversations we had while riding bikes were nothing momentous, but he made me feel that I counted. I was worth his time. That feeling was a bulwark against future events and experiences that could easily undermine a girl's confidence, even when everyone else accepted them as normal. When my father spent time with me, he was not drawing a direct line to law, or to anything in particular. He was, however, giving me raw material—activity and emotion—from which I could shape life for myself.

2

Walking the Color Line
Muriel Petioni, Physician
(b. 1914)

When Muriel Petioni walked down the ship's gangway onto the pier at Ellis Island, her father stood waiting. He had been gone from Trinidad for a year, and she was ecstatic to see him, to feel his arms around her. She was impatient for the processing to be completed and the luggage sorted so that he could take them—her mother, Rosa, her sister Marguerite, and her—to the Harlem apartment he had ready. It was 1919, and Muriel was five years old—too young to read the literature of the Harlem Renaissance, or appreciate that the women's suffrage movement was approaching its crescendo, or discern which doors in her new country would be open to her and her family and which closed. But she was old enough to absorb her parents' optimism that better opportunities lay ahead and that Harlem was the place to find them.

Muriel was Dahlov Ipcar's contemporary, just three years older. They grew up only a subway ride apart: Dahlov enmeshed in the lively modern art world of Greenwich Village, Muriel surrounded by Harlem's own dynamic culture. When they eventually embarked on their distinctive careers, in art and in medicine, their paths were shaped by unique family dynamics, their parents' circle of friends, education, current events—and race.

ILLUS. 2.1 Muriel Petioni as a young girl in Trinidad, undated. Photograph courtesy of Charles Woolfolk.

I first heard about Muriel at a conference when I described my book to an acquaintance. You really should interview this doctor in Harlem, she said, and offered to make an introduction. When I followed up with a phone call, Muriel immediately said yes. She added, emphatically, that we would talk about race. She must have assumed I was white, or my acquaintance told her I was, and that I would benefit from hearing how race was part of her experience. She was spot-on. I did want frank talk about the impact of race on a professional woman's path. Muriel was my energetic guide to a new understanding.[1]

On a windy day in February, I took the bus from Boston's Back Bay station to New York's Port Authority, caught the A train to 135th Street, and walked the several blocks to Muriel's apartment. When I stepped off the elevator, she was standing at the open door, dressed in a lilac-colored pantsuit, multicolored carved cane in hand, pewter hair curled under at the chin. Inside, sunlight streamed through the windows. African masks hung on the living room wall, and stacks of books about Harlem lay on the table in front of the sofa. "You can't talk to me if we don't talk about my father," she said as prelude, before she launched into the story of Charles Petioni—ambitious immigrant, distinguished doctor, committed activist.

Charles grew up in Trinidad when it was a British colony. As a young man, he worked as a journalist, writing about the dark side of colonial rule and advocating for West Indian independence. The British authorities tolerated him for only so long. When they "invited him to leave," as Muriel put it, echoing the polite-sounding British expression for expulsion, Charles formulated a plan: he would emigrate to the United States, attend medical school, and fight for independence from abroad. Medicine, he believed, was a "liberating profession" through which he could say what he thought without being threatened, blackballed, or forced to leave his home. He was hardly naive about the discrimination he would face in the United States, but he was optimistic.

In New York, he headed for Harlem and found manual labor jobs. A year later, he sent for his family, and when he met them at Ellis Island, he had a railroad apartment waiting. Here Muriel interjected: "I don't know if you know about railroad apartments." She wanted me to visualize the long, narrow configuration of rooms that later would house both the family and her father's first medical office.

Harlem was flush with new arrivals and hope. Black residents had lived there for generations, a minority among the white majority. When racial animus increased in other parts of the city, particularly around 1900, many Black New Yorkers found Harlem a safer place to live.[2]

Over the next two decades, Caribbean immigrants arrived in Harlem, along with African Americans desperate to escape the Jim Crow South, part of the Great Migration. The new arrivals, together with native New Yorkers, transformed Harlem. It was never more "high-spirited and engaging than it was during the nineteen-twenties," wrote Jervis Anderson in his book *This Was Harlem*. "Blacks from all over America and the Caribbean were pouring in, reviving the migration that had abated toward the end of the war—word having reached them about the 'city,' in the heart of Manhattan, that blacks were making their own."[3]

By 1920, a stretch of 135th Street was populated by Black-owned businesses—groceries; butchers; restaurants; barbershops and beauty parlors; dress and shoe shops; drugstores; real estate and employment agencies; furniture movers; ice, coal, and wood dealers. Professional offices also proliferated. As Eslanda Goode Robeson wrote in her book about her husband, singer and actor Paul Robeson, Harlem had "a complete life of its own. There were young and old Negro physicians and dentists, with much larger practices than they could comfortably look after themselves; Negroes owned beautiful houses and modern apartments; there were many fine churches; . . . there were Negro graduates from the finest white universities in America; there were Negroes in every conceivable profession, business, and trade."[4]

This is not to say that all Harlem businesses were Black-owned—far from it. Many businesses had white owners, and they often reserved the better-paying jobs for white employees, a disparity that later gave rise to pickets and boycotts.[5] There were other disparities too. Migrants from the South often had little education, and their job experience was primarily in agriculture. For them, the path to the middle class would be longer and more arduous than it was for Muriel's family.

As the family settled into Harlem, Muriel and her sister went to the local public school while their father walked to City College, a few blocks away, for premed classes. Muriel herself never studied there, but many decades later, the college presented her with an award for public service. It was only one of many honors she received, including from Barnard College and Howard University, but she found the school's idealism particularly moving. "City College really favored immigrants. No tuition. All you had to do was buy books and appear. The sky was the limit as far as what you could achieve."

When her father completed his premed classes, it was nearly inevitable that he would leave the family again. The chance he would be accepted by a "white" medical school was much lower than his chances of acceptance at Howard University in Washington, D.C., or at Meharry Medical College in Nashville, Tennessee. As Howard explains on its website, "until the 1960's, Howard and Meharry trained most of the African-American physicians of this nation. For most of the first half of the twentieth century, many medical schools (including all medical schools in the South except Meharry) did not accept black students." When Howard said yes, how could he say no?[6]

Howard was among the more prestigious of the historically black colleges and universities (HBCUs) that had sprung up around the time of the Civil War. A few HBCUs began before the war, but most, including Howard, came after, often founded under church auspices, with the help of the Freedmen's Bureau, or pursuant to federal legislation.[7] The impact was and remains extensive: three-quarters of all Black persons with a doctoral degree, three-quarters of all Black officers in the armed forces, and four-fifths of all Black federal judges are HBCU graduates.[8] Our country's first woman vice president graduated from Howard. As Ta-Nehisi Coates writes in *Between the World and Me*, Howard is notable for its graduate programs but even more so for its energetic support of Black community life.[9] This was something that Charles Petioni and, later, Muriel would experience firsthand.

I try to imagine a conversation between Muriel's parents

about having to live apart again. Should the family move with him? How would they manage in New York? What could they afford? In the end, I believe it was not a difficult decision. Her father's plan to become a doctor was really a plan for the whole family. Furthermore, they were already settled in New York. As Muriel told me, "all of our support system was here in New York City. There was a whole Caribbean community of people from Jamaica, Barbados, and the Bahamas. We were strangers in a strange land, so we bonded. Anybody who was from the Caribbean, those were our people. And if you were from Trinidad, you were really our people."

From the vantage point of her ninety-three years, Muriel understood why her father went away for school. She knew all about the ways that race defined educational and employment opportunities. But as a young girl, she must have hated his leaving. They had already spent a year apart, and this separation would be longer. Her mother would keep family life grounded in New York.

In Trinidad, Muriel's mother had apprenticed to a dressmaker, and in New York, she found a job in a clothing factory. "My mother worked in the garment industry as a finisher," Muriel told me. What exactly did that entail? "I never asked her, but I assumed it was when the garment was pretty much finished, she would cut the threads and do other little things."

Muriel's hunch was essentially correct. A finisher attended to the hem, buttons, and decoration of a garment during the last stage of the manufacturing process. It was one of the few jobs her mother could have gotten in the industry. According to historian Irma Watkins-Owens, Black women "accounted for less than 2 percent of the International Ladies Garment Workers Union in 1929 and were practically unknown as cutters and operators—the key crafts. Most served as finishers at the lower end of the wage scale."[10]

If the union had been open to promoting Black women, maybe Rosa would have advanced to another job with better pay. But it wasn't, and she didn't. Unlike Dahlov Ipcar's mother, who was interviewed by a newspaper about options for women artists, Rosa left no public record of what she thought about opportunities for women like her.

With their mother at work, Muriel and her sister spent time after school at a neighbor's house. Shortly before five, they were allowed to walk home. "Maybe three-quarters of an hour before Mama was due," Muriel said, "we would let ourselves into the apartment and wait for her to come home. Maybe we'd start dinner. We were latchkey children, but not so much that we were alone the whole day."

Having an adult present when the children were around was standard protocol for the family. Muriel's father was adamant about it. "We played with everyone on the block when we were growing up," she said, "but when we got a little older and were invited to people's houses, my father was very careful about who we played with. He would say, 'What does the father do? What does the brother do? Who lives in the house? I am going to go and meet them and find out what kind of house this is.'"

When Charles finished medical school, an internship at Harlem Hospital would have been ideal. But that was not possible in 1925. As Muriel explained, "Black people couldn't intern at any of the white hospitals, or any of the large hospitals, so we interned at Black-owned hospitals throughout the country. There were maybe a dozen well-recognized Black-run hospitals where we could finish from." Her father became an intern at Saint Agnes Hospital in Raleigh, North Carolina, located on the campus of Saint Augustine College, an HBCU.[11]

A year later, back in New York, he was ready to start his own medical practice. The two front rooms of the family's railroad apartment were set aside for patients, the back rooms for family. Charles made his new practice known to an established physician who lived on the next block. "I hope if you need any help," he said to the older man when he paid a visit, "you would allow me to be of help. And if you have any house calls that you don't want to make, I would be glad to make them for you—night calls, house calls, whatever." I imagine Charles sitting in his neighbor's parlor, dressed in a suit and tie. "Of course this was British courtesy," Muriel told me. "You did that kind of thing."

With the medical practice under way, Muriel's mother gave up her factory job. She became the "receptionist, housekeeper and jack-of-all-trades," Muriel said. "Once my father finished school, he needed her at home, and we needed her at home."

A brownstone building on West 131st Street became the family's home within a few years, thanks to the growing medical practice and some of Charles's business investments. It had an office suite, separate family quarters, and extra rooms to rent to friends and relatives as they arrived from the Caribbean, and it suited all their needs. "That's the way immigrants did it, in case you don't know," Muriel continued. "They rented and then got apartments that they shared with other people who were coming over and needed a thing. And most of the guys I knew—my father and his group who were immigrants—they bought houses as soon as they got on their feet. And they did the same thing—had the office in one part of the house, lived in another, and rented out rooms until they got established. Then they took over more of the house."

The brownstone was the center of what Muriel called the "family medical practice." She didn't mean just her father and, eventually, herself; she was talking about seven uncles and cousins who also were doctors and for whom the brownstone was a gathering place. The house was also a hub for friends and colleagues from Charles's many civic and business activities. He was a cofounder of Carver Bank, which continues to this day. He helped start a local medical association and became a convincing public spokesperson on health issues. He continued to push for Caribbean independence and supported a pan-African movement, which earned him the honor of being doctor to Marcus Garvey and a political colleague of W. E. B. Du Bois.[12]

When her father's colleagues came to the house, Muriel listened in. Their conversation was educated and passionate. "I grew up in a well-read, intelligent family," she said. "All our friends and associates had educations, and most of my father's associates were professional men: lawyers, doctors, and ministers. This is the kind of people I grew up around. Very middle class."

She also was a close observer of his medical practice. When she was home from school, she rushed to answer the phone and ushered patients into the waiting room. These were small things, but enough to suggest an on-ramp to a career. "Living in the house with my father, answering the door and telephone, mingling with the patients, I got the feeling that this would be

ILLUS. 2.2 The Petioni family (*clockwise,* Charles, Julio, Rosa, Muriel, and Marguerite), circa 1933. Photograph courtesy of Charles Woolfolk.

nice to do. I think I can do this. I was just an average student. I didn't have any particular talent, not like my sister. She had a nice singing voice, a natural. She played violin in the school orchestra. She was gregarious, popular. I didn't have that, but I thought it might be nice to go into medicine."

Conjure, if you will, a young Muriel immersed in the goings-on at home—the medical practice, the debates about global politics and conversations about racial justice. Think of Dahlov Ipcar at the same age, paying close attention as her parents create their paintings and sculptures. Each girl is wrapped up in the family's line of work and wondering whether she wants to continue it. Both have exceptionally engaged fathers and, in Dahlov's case, a mother with her own career. Muriel's mother plays a different role, energetically entwined with her husband's activities.

After I met Muriel, I spoke with her son Charles Woolfolk. He elaborated on his grandmother's role as confidante and advisor to her husband. She was in charge of the administrative side of the medical practice, orchestrated the schedule for her husband's many meetings, and managed the rental of the brownstone's top floors. I came to understand her as someone involved with the issues and activities, but with a more private persona. What Muriel had said—"he needed her at home, and we needed her at home"—was an understatement.

Central to the family's aspirations was education. As Muriel's father told her, "'your grandfather was a college graduate, your father was a college graduate, and you've got to be a college graduate too.' That was part of our society, so to speak, our family society. And my father was equal opportunity. His daughters were going to be as educated as any boy in the family." The boy in the family to whom she referred was Julio, her half brother from her father's previous relationship. "He didn't come over with us, but he came later, when he was in high school. His mother wanted my father to educate him."

Charles underscored his message about education when he introduced Muriel to members of the esteemed Delany family. She was in junior high school, already thinking she would go into medicine, when they walked over to Seventh Avenue, between 135th and 136th Streets, to an office shared by several of the adult children of Henry Beard Delany. Charles knew Bishop Delany from his time in North Carolina. The older man had been born into slavery in Georgia and, after the Civil War, achieved distinction in multiple disciplines. He was a teacher at Saint Augustine College, the designer of the college chapel, and a bishop of the Episcopal Church—the first Black man in North Carolina and the second in the country to hold that position. His ten children had impressive careers in education, law, medicine, and dentistry. Several lived in New York, and these were the people Charles wanted Muriel to meet.

She remembered sitting in their office. "So there we were with four professional Black people. Two of them women. Women! For a long time, if a Black woman went on to college, she went into nursing or teaching. There weren't too many going into other professions. This was really significant that I got to meet other professionals." Muriel reminded me that two of the sisters, Sarah and Bessie, a teacher and a dentist, published a shared memoir when they were 103 and 101 years old, respectively.[13]

Not only was this meeting important to Muriel but hearing about it shifted something in my thinking as well. Slavery is not so very far away in our country's history. Muriel's father knew a man born into slavery, Muriel met his children, and I met Muriel. This was a reminder that slavery is not something to be studied in school and then consigned to the bin of "long ago"; it is closer to us today than we like to think.

For high school, Muriel and her sister went to the nearby Wadleigh School, called the "finest high school building in the world" when it opened in 1902. The *New York Times* described its "eighty classrooms, over a dozen laboratories, executive offices, two elevators, three gymnasia, an auditorium, a library, a large boiler and engine room, two study halls, and numerous lavatories and cloakrooms." The curriculum was equally outstanding. "Every branch of learning has a place. Botany, biology, chemistry, drawing, cooking—nothing is left out." There were three thousand students, all girls, who came from all over the city, including, as the *Times* reported, "a few negroes, about two in each class on an average."[14] The racial composition was about the same, Muriel told me, when she was a student some twenty years later.

Muriel thought I might recognize the name Wadleigh, and I should have, because Lydia Fowler Wadleigh was a pioneer in female education. Originally from New Hampshire, she was principal of New York's first public school for girls that went beyond the primary grades. When she took the job in 1856, anything beyond primary school was considered "higher" education. When it came to girls, it was still a controversial idea. Those who preached against it used two inconsistent arguments: education for girls was pointless because they were intellectually inferior, but on the other hand, if they got a taste of it, they would indulge their intellects and abandon their duties at home. The *Times* weighed in in favor of the proposed school:

> We cannot now stop to argue those relics of an age gone by, who still insist, in the face of all experience and common sense, that the female intelligence is essentially inferior to our own, and therefore not susceptible to an equal degree of cultivation. Still less do we propose to deal with the wretched assumption that it is inexpedient to give young ladies a finished education, lest it should unfit them for the discharge of those domestic duties which pertain to their sex.[15]

(Reading this, I laughed to see the concession that female intellect is not inferior to "our own"—a reminder of who ran the paper.)

Lydia Wadleigh was a champion for the girls in her charge, and that included Mary Putnam, daughter of the prominent publisher George Putnam. Mary liked science, even though her father thought it an inappropriate subject for girls, and Wadleigh encouraged her. When Mary later graduated from medical school in 1864, she was an outspoken advocate for a scientific approach in medicine, which the field sorely lacked at the time. Wadleigh herself went on to be superintendent of New York City's Normal College, which Thomas Hunter founded in 1870 to train young women to be teachers. It was the precursor to today's Hunter College.

Muriel began her college studies at New York University, where she took premed classes. But when she was a sophomore, her father suggested a transfer. She would stand a better chance of getting into Howard's medical school if she was already on campus as an undergraduate. She took his advice, and the

ILLUS. 2.3   Muriel Petioni as an intern at Harlem Hospital, circa 1937. Photograph courtesy of Charles Woolfolk.

strategy was successful. Muriel was the only woman in the class of 1937 at Howard University College of Medicine.

As a Black woman, Muriel had mastered a very narrow path to get that far. No more than 5 percent of medical students in the country were women. Some schools did not admit women at all, and others used quotas to limit their number. Furthermore, race meant that the odds of her being accepted at a so-called white medical school were lower than they were for white women.[16]

Thinking about intersectionality, I asked Muriel about what some call the "double bind" of race and gender. Obviously, she was well aware of the challenges she had faced throughout her life in education and employment, but she did not see herself as disadvantaged. "I grew up in a middle-class professional family. The people around us were educated, well read. My father said all you have to do is study—I'll find the money to send you to school. He wasn't making a lot of money but enough from his practice and his investments to send three of us to higher education, two of us in medicine and one through her master's." With this family background and socioeconomic class, she and her siblings had what they needed to overcome daunting odds. That, she said, "got rid of some of the Black woman stuff."

By the time she graduated from medical school in 1937, one change had occurred that worked in her favor: Harlem Hospital had opened its internship program to young Black doctors, and that is where she interned. "A lot of people think I was the first Black female to intern at Harlem, but I wasn't. That was Dr. May Edward Chinn in 1926." Still, it was rare that a woman interned anywhere. In 1940, New York City hospitals offered more than one thousand internships, but only forty-two were held by women.[17]

Desegregating the medical staff at Harlem Hospital was a process marked by steps and missteps, actions and reactions. When the hospital hired Dr. Louis Wright, its first Black doctor, in 1919, he had impressive credentials—fourth in his class at Harvard Medical School, training at Bellevue Hospital, service during World War I that earned him the Purple Heart. Despite his record, he was slotted as a lowly clinical assistant, several white physicians resigned in protest, and the doctor who hired him was demoted.[18]

When the neighborhood rallied for more Black doctors, Mayor James Walker felt the political pressure and initiated a hospital reorganization to accommodate the demand. "The precedent was set," Muriel said, "that from now on they would admit a certain number of Black interns, including women. Black interns, OK? That was money in the bank. Long before anybody else in New York City or anywhere else, in Harlem you were guaranteed that in every year they would take four or five or six Black interns."[19]

Even with more Black doctors, some Harlem residents preferred to stay with the white doctors they were used to. As she explained, "people in Harlem who had money still went to white doctors. White doctors were *the* doctors. White people knew more than Black people. People who went to Harvard and Princeton and Columbia knew more than those who went to Howard. That was the perception."

When she finished her internship, Muriel moved to Saint Louis, a segregated city with segregated medical facilities, for a residency at the Homer G. Phillips Hospital, a new facility dedicated to caring for Black patients and training Black doctors and nurses. She planned to specialize in ob-gyn, but within a few months, her father called—he had found a job for her. "A residency is OK, but I've got two kids behind you to educate, and I think you ought to take this job and help me out financially." He knew the president of Wilberforce University in Ohio, and the school had an opening for a campus physician. Muriel agreed—"it was OK with me," she said—and moved to what would be the first of several posts at HBCUs. After a year at Wilberforce, she took a job at Alabama State Teachers College in Montgomery.

To get an idea of what Montgomery was like at the time, I searched microfilm copies of the local newspaper, the *Montgomery Advertiser*. After the attack on Pearl Harbor, the paper kept tabs on local men who enlisted. If they were white, the paper printed their names and hometowns. When Black men enlisted, no particulars were given, only a generic caption, such as "Seventeen Negroes Inducted." A local technical school advertised a defense training course that was "free to any white person in Alabama" with a high school education. As Muriel reminded me, Montgomery was the cradle of the Confederacy, where the plan to secede was hatched. Eighty years later, when she lived there, the system of white supremacy was fully operational and legal. From a nearly endless list of laws and regulations, I cite only a few: white nurses were prohibited from tending to Black male patients; places of public accommodation were required to have separate facilities; and race mixing was banned, even over a friendly game of checkers.[20]

While in Montgomery, Muriel met Mallalieu Woolfolk, known as Mal. "I was at Alabama State Teachers College when I met my husband," she said. "He had come down south from the University of Minnesota, where he earned his master's in educational psychology. He was teaching at Alabama State, while waiting to be called up for the service. I got a job at Bennett College, in Greensboro, North Carolina, and at the same time he was called up. We got married on the way to North Carolina. It was just one of those things."

One of those things? Maybe so. A lot of couples were marrying quickly as men headed off to war. In Muriel's case, the marriage lasted more than twenty years and produced a son, but she was not keen to talk about it. Her son Charles filled me in. "It was like they were two big personalities, together in a room. She was similar in spirit to her father, which meant she knew her mind and wanted to get somewhere. And my father was also a strong character, always stirring something up."

Mal had grown up in Mississippi, the son of a Methodist minister who taught at Rust College in Holly Springs. "When my father got into trouble in school," Charles said, "his parents did not tolerate it well. He moved to Saint Louis to live with his aunt and then to Chicago to live with an uncle, where he worked in the stockyards, and as a railroad porter and in clubs." Eventually, he graduated from Lincoln University in Missouri, and then from the University of Minnesota. Soon after he and Muriel were married, he was on his way to Europe to serve with the Tuskegee Airmen as a logistics officer.

While Mal was away, Muriel worked at Bennett College, and then at Hampton Institute in Virginia. At the same time, she contemplated her future. "I was thinking that my next step would be to take a degree in public health or in psychiatry. But then the war ended, and my husband was coming home. When he got back, he wanted to go to Chicago because his family was there, so I went to Chicago and became a housewife for four years."

For the first time in our conversation, Muriel described herself as having lost focus. "I knew I'd have to take the state licensing exam, and that I didn't want to do. I had passed the exam in New York and had reciprocity with some other states, but I would have had to practice in Illinois for a year before I qualified for the exam, and I didn't feel like it. My days consisted of getting up late, looking at the soap operas and getting myself presentable in time for my husband to come home. I'd fix dinner. I had no social life, really. The one or two professional people I knew wouldn't associate with me because I was just a housewife. My husband was in law school at DePaul, and he had various jobs, the kind you get when you're in school. Then I had my son Charles, in 1947."

Her family in New York must have known she was struggling to find her footing. They may have thought she needed a push. "Toward the end of that four-year period, my father sent an older cousin to talk to me," Muriel said. "This cousin had finished medical school in 1930, and he made a special trip to Chicago to get me back to New York." Her father wanted to introduce her and Mal to his connections, to help them get established in Harlem. "You've wasted enough time sitting around here being a housewife," her cousin told her. "You need to come back to New York. Now."

Muriel heard her cousin out, then she went to Mal. "I decided it was time, so I told my husband I was moving. He said, 'What, you're going to leave me for a year?' But you know how these men are. I came back to New York in 1950. My son came back with me. My mother could take care of him, because she was at home. My husband stayed in Chicago for a year or so before he followed me."

Being back in Harlem renewed her energy. "My cousin had established an office in Harlem, and I worked out of his office for a while. I shadowed people, to get myself reestablished in the medical field. And I took other jobs too. At first, I volunteered in a clinic to get some additional experience." Then, with her years of experience working with students, she got a job in the city's Department of Health as a school physician.

Mal joined Muriel and their son Charles in Harlem as soon as he graduated and went into law practice with Percy Sutton, a tent-mate from the army. That firm's lawyers would go on to play a prominent role in New York's legal and political circles, representing Malcolm X and other activists, and Sutton himself being elected Manhattan borough president. In addition, Mal had a business consulting firm, a liquor store, and a data processing company. As Charles recalled, "data processing in those days involved punch cards. Remember those? I used to carry parcels of them on the subway, from one of my father's locations to the next."

Charles described his mother's workday as well. "She would begin at eight in the morning in the schools and in the afternoon see patients in her office until seven o'clock, with just a short break." She had taken over the office in the family brownstone after her father died and secured admitting privileges at Harlem Hospital. "Many nights, my mother worked much later. As long as you got in the door before seven, she would see you, even if she didn't get to you until later. Some of her patients had been her father's, and they were quite old, unable to get about easily. She would go visit them in their homes, often walk-up apartments. Often they had no insurance and not much money. Her payment would be a cup of soup or a sandwich."

Muriel became known both for her generosity to patients and for her broad interpretation of a physician's role. Whether or not they asked for it, she gave her patients advice on nutrition and exercise. Eventually, whenever they saw her, they knew what was coming.

In the schools, she also used an expansive job definition. When a struggling student came to her attention, she would convene a conference with the teacher, the guidance counselor, and the case worker, if there was one. As she told me, she knew she was conspicuous as a Black woman physician, particularly after she became a supervisor, and she used her status to be an advocate. "Kids need someone who will push them and encourage them and tell them they can do it. If it's parents, they're lucky. But if it's not a parent, it could be a teacher or a neighbor or somebody who will take them under their wing and say you can become great someday. And tell them there's a bigger world than central Harlem."

In her private practice, house calls were expected, just as when her father had begun his practice, but Muriel had other reasons to make them. Some of her elderly patients could not easily come to her. She also wanted to be the woman who met or exceeded expectations. "I felt as a woman physician I had to be extra special and do house calls. Otherwise, men would say that women just weren't as good." Whenever she was called, she went, until a cab driver told her to think again. "One night I called a cab to take me to a patient, someone I knew, at two in the morning. 'What are you doing out at this time?' the cab driver said. I explained I was a doctor, making a house call. 'You don't need to be doing that,' he told me. 'Even the men aren't doing it anymore.' He was right in a way, but Harlem is like a village. It's always been like that, and we all look after each other. And there were not many physicians in those days, so people really looked after each other. But this man was right. It was OK to make house calls during the day, but not in the middle of the night."[21]

The cabbie's advice reflected changes that had occurred in Harlem. The buoyant spirit of the 1920s had evaporated, replaced by a hard reality that Jervis Anderson describes:

> If Black Harlem was once a heaven, or was seen to be one by the migrants and the commentators of the 1920s, it had ceased to be that by the beginning of the 1950s. When the early optimism had been exhausted, there remained, among the majority of the population, almost all the racial and social hardships that many had hoped would be nonexistent in the finest urban community that blacks had ever occupied in the United States.[22]

Muriel added that drugs further disrupted the community. "Things didn't get bad until drugs came in, in the late fifties, early sixties. That's when the Mafia just dumped these drugs in Harlem," she said.

Faced with a changing neighborhood, Muriel and Mal decided to move to Teaneck, New Jersey. They would work in Harlem, but live ten miles away. "It was our flight to the suburbs. We were among the first Blacks to move into Teaneck. We thought the schools would be better for our son," she told me.

There they found a different world. One Black couple, whom they happened to know, moved in across the street, but the town was overwhelmingly white. And Muriel was torn. "In my social life, I was Mrs. Woolfolk. But professionally, I kept the name Petioni. I had finished medical school with that name, plus the name was known in Harlem. That's where my father practiced, and everyone knew the name."

In 1970, when her son finished school, Muriel made another change. Again, she was succinct. "I left my husband because we weren't getting along. I left him in the house with my son, and his aunt who was taking care of the household, and I came back to New York. I had my practice here. I had my building here. My life was in Harlem."

Indeed. In Harlem, her professional life thrived. Until she was close to seventy, she continued working in the schools and maintained her private practice. And her community involvement only deepened. She was active with the Manhattan Central Medical Society, the Greater Harlem Chamber of Commerce, the Harlem Council of Elders, and the Harlem Congregations for Community Improvement (which named its senior living complex for her). Perhaps her biggest contribution was at the hospital. As founder of the Friends of Harlem Hospital Center, she turned the Friends into a significant fund-raising enterprise. She also advised the hospital on its expansion of pediatric and geriatric services and the hospital honored her by naming its new boardroom and geriatric wing for her.

Her drive was incredible. When I remarked on that, she explained that the energy of her whole family had become concentrated in her. Not only had her parents died but so had her sister and brother. Marguerite had graduated from Smith College with a master's degree in social work and was working out in the field when she came down with a fatal case of spinal tuberculosis. Julio was a student at Meharry Medical College when he died of hemophilia. As Muriel said, "I lost my sister and my brother when they were young adults. I had to take on the family legacy."

She was also active beyond Harlem. As part of the Coalition of 100 Black Women, she helped establish a mentoring program for young women interested in medicine and science. Within the National Medical Association (NMA), she started a group for women doctors.

The NMA began in 1895, when Black doctors were excluded from the larger, older American Medical Association (AMA). To be a member of the AMA, a doctor had to belong to a local medical society. But many local groups discouraged or outright refused membership to Black doctors, with the predictable result that the AMA was a mostly white organization. At the NMA, like everywhere else, most of the doctors were male, and they rarely focused on their female colleagues. Then Muriel

ILLUS. 2.4 Muriel Petioni with her son Charles Woolfolk and daughter-in-law Carol Dixon-Woolfolk at a Harlem Hospital gala, circa 2008. Photograph courtesy of Charles Woolfolk.

got involved. She convened a small group to talk about issues faced by women in practice. Within a few years, the group had ballooned to hundreds, large enough to host Maya Angelou as the keynote speaker at a meeting. Today, the Council on Concerns of Women Physicians continues and, at its annual event, presents an award in Muriel's name.[23]

But Muriel saw yet another way to help Black women advance in the profession. "It was the 1970s, and affirmative action had already come in," she explained. "Black doctors were being hired, but maybe one or two here and another one there. There weren't enough in any one place to make a group, and they weren't welcome in the white groups, so they were isolated. At the same time, people knew my name from the NMA, and they started writing to me, asking me to recommend Black women for jobs. I thought I could help by organizing women so they would know each other, and I could know them and make referrals.

"I went to some of my contemporaries, and we drew up a list of women, maybe a hundred of them, who were practicing in the greater New York area and invited them to a meeting. This was in 1974." The group became known as the Susan Smith McKinney Steward Medical Society, named after the first African American woman to earn a medical degree in the state of New York.

Dr. Steward had started her career in 1870, treating women and children and founding several medical clinics. She advocated for women's suffrage and against the lynching of Black people, but she and Muriel were connected in another way. She ended her long career as the campus physician at Wilberforce University, where Muriel began hers.

Muriel described the group's first meeting. "Forty women showed up, from Connecticut, New Jersey, and many of us from New York City. And these young gals came with long hair hanging down their backs, polished fingernails and toenails, in open-toe sandals. High-heeled open-toe sandals! Looking like women. We, the older ones, looked like women, but we were staid and very professional. These gals were so sure of themselves in the field of medicine that they walked around in painted toenails. We were so proud of them."

Nail polish on the toes—was this superficial or a sign of

something deeper? For Muriel, it showed that medicine was becoming more hospitable to women.

"In my day, to make it as a woman professional, you had to be very conservative. The men were kind of prejudiced against us anyway, and if you looked too feminine, they wouldn't make referrals or respect you. Even patients had a certain picture of doctors, which meant they had a hard time envisioning women doctors. We had to be doctors first and women second. But these women were women first and doctors second."

In 2019 Dr. Patrice Harris was elected president of the AMA, the first Black woman to fill that position. Muriel did not live to see that happen, but I think she would have been thrilled to see a Black woman succeed at something that was inconceivable only a generation before—and that Dr. Harris is often photographed with styled hair, fashionable clothes, and, yes, nail polish.

I had arrived at Muriel's apartment just after noon, in bright sunlight. As we talked, I watched the light turn golden. By four o'clock on that winter afternoon, the sun was beginning to set. Muriel, however, was not fading. "Here, let me show you my isometric exercises," she said, lifting her arms. "I do them every morning. You should do them too." I raised my arms and held them overhead, tightening my muscles, feeling their internal pressure. Would this, I wondered, give me energy remotely comparable to hers?

The battery in my recorder had already given out. Without a spare, I had resorted to scribbling notes, trying to keep up with her words. But now that we were doing isometric exercises, I gave up writing entirely. I followed her lead until I gave her my thanks and walked to the subway in the waning light.

As I meandered, I reflected on Muriel's prediction that we would talk about race when we met. She had proved to be right. We had not always talked about it in explicit terms; the subject was simply embedded in our conversation. The neighborhood where she lived, the university she attended, the places she worked, the organizations to which she dedicated her time—all were integral to her experience of being Black, female, and a doctor.

I had come to the interview with certain of my own perceptions and misperceptions. She opened my eyes to the reality of
segregated health care. For that, I was grateful, and for her giving
me the incentive to learn about Harlem's history.

W. E. B. Du Bois once wrote that "the problem of the twentieth century is the problem of the Color Line." Racial differences
were and would be the reason people were denied the right to
share in opportunities and privileges.[24] Muriel found that to be
true when she walked along that line, a result that was immoral,
even if legal at the time. But the color line did not defeat her. She
found common cause with others, and that gave her strength.
She became known as "the mother of medicine in Harlem," as
both the *Amsterdam News* and the *New York Times* noted, a tribute
to the way she lived out a legacy.

Fourth-Grade Fantasy

In fourth grade, the teacher gave us an assignment: pick a job you would like to do and tell the class about it. Unlike Muriel Petioni, who started thinking about medicine as soon as she saw what went on in her father's medical office, I hadn't given any thought to future jobs, except I figured I would have one. But faced with this assignment, I decided I wanted to be on television, giving the nightly news.

I forget exactly what I told the class, but I surely talked about Chet Huntley and David Brinkley. My parents watched their news broadcast every evening. If I wandered in when the TV was on, I noticed the aura of authority and low-key yet suave style emanating from the screen. Serious about the news, the pair seemed not to take themselves too seriously. It sounds grandiose to say that a fourth grader thought she might become an authority who made it look easy, but that is how I saw myself in a glittering, imagined future.

No woman anchored a news show. ABC newsman Ron Cochran had not yet come down with laryngitis, as he did in 1964, when Marlene Sanders filled in and became the first woman to anchor a network newscast. Judy Woodruff, Diane Sawyer, and Connie Chung were still teenagers when I was in fourth grade, and Gwen Ifill was younger than I was.

I never made it to television. In high school, I wrote news and opinion pieces for the school paper and was an editor. At Oberlin, I read the news on the college radio station. I was surprised, though, at how easily I stumbled, particularly when announcing sports scores at the end of each broadcast. Humbled by my performance, I concluded that I was not cut out to be a news anchor. I gave up before I tried to get better.

But still, I clung to a vision of myself as someone who would be respected for her knowledge and authority. The catch was that I had no idea how I would turn that vision into reality.

3

A Unique Wartime Opportunity

Cordelia Dodson Hood,
Intelligence Officer

(b. 1913)

Sunday, December 7, 1941. Americans are wrapping up their weekends, enjoying a midday dinner, resting on the sofa, listening to the radio. Suddenly, news flashes interrupt the regular programming. Pearl Harbor has been attacked.

Hours later, First Lady Eleanor Roosevelt comes on the radio, just as she does every Sunday. This evening, she casts aside her planned remarks to speak about the attack, the first person associated with the administration to do so. The president, she says, is meeting with his advisors; they will report to Congress in the morning. She does not say that her husband has crafted his speech about this "day which will live in infamy" and that he plans to ask Congress for a declaration of war, but everyone knows what's coming. Instead, she talks to the women of America:

> I should like to say just a word to the women in the country tonight. I have a boy at sea on a destroyer; for all I know he may be on his way to the Pacific. Two of my children are in

coast cities on the Pacific. Many of you all over the country
have boys in the services who will now be called upon to
go into action. You have friends and families in what has
suddenly become a danger zone. You cannot escape anxiety.
You cannot escape a clutch of fear at your heart, and yet I
hope that the certainty of what we have to meet will make
you rise above these fears.[1]

Cordelia Dodson understood Mrs. Roosevelt's purpose, even
if the words were not aimed at her. Cordelia was twenty-seven,
was unmarried, and had no son in the service. She did not need
to have the urgency explained. She had spent nearly two years
in Europe after college. In Munich, she saw brown-shirted men
patrol the streets. She was in Vienna when the Germans crossed
the border into Austria. One of her friends, an Austrian Jew, was
abducted and imprisoned in Dachau. When news of Pearl Harbor
broke, Cordelia understood the stakes, and she knew she would
take action, even if she didn't know how.

She was at a crossroads. Her mother had recently died, and
the family's big house in Milwaukie, Oregon, where she had
grown up, was sold. She was living in Washington, D.C., where
her father worked for Oregon's senator Charles McNarry. With
a master's degree in German, she was thinking she might get an
advanced degree in linguistics. She loved languages, but a life in
academia seemed to lack excitement. Unlike Dahlov Ipcar and
Muriel Petioni, who knew as teenagers what they wanted to do,
Cordelia waffled, undecided, until the attack on Pearl Harbor
gave her a jolt that more studying never could.

I knew the broad outlines of Cordelia's life before we sat
down for an interview. She was a friend of my husband's family.
From them I heard stories of her wartime work for the Office of
Strategic Services (OSS) and, later, for the Central Intelligence
Agency. My husband and I saw her in Damariscotta, Maine,
where she lived in retirement, when we were nearby at our
summer cottage. Now I was in her den, about to dive into the
past, to learn how she became an intelligence officer in what was
very much a man's world.

Not long before this interview, my family had visited
Washington, D.C., where I took my son to the International

Spy Museum. One exhibit featured Mata Hari, the exotic dancer executed for espionage during the First World War. She exemplified a well-known version of a female spy, one who used her body to advantage. Cordelia was different. An analytical mind and quick wits, not sex, were at the root of her tradecraft—more John le Carré than Ian Fleming.

Finding a time to get together was not easy. Cordelia and her sister Lisbeth, who lived in the house next to hers, had been hosting guests all summer. Cordelia also was taking continuing education classes. "So much poetry has been written since I graduated from college that I have a lot of catching up to do," she told me. "And the scholarship of the Founding Fathers has expanded, with new biographies and studies written in the last seventy years, so early American history is worth studying all over again." But in late August, when the summer guests were gone, she made time for me. She was then ninety-three.

From my chair in her den, I looked out the window to see a pool of calm, green water at the head of the Damariscotta River before it rushed toward the ocean. A small boat bobbed at its mooring. Books were stacked on the table in front of me, with that morning's newspaper open on top. On the sofa next to Cordelia was a stack of books about Renaissance architecture. She was going to the Veneto in the fall to visit Palladian villas. On the corner of the table rested a pad with a list written in, not shorthand exactly, but a kind of speed writing she had learned at OSS. This interview would turn out to be one of two, which I supplemented by talking to her sister Lisbeth, her niece Sarah, friends, and her ex-husband.

Because her prewar experience in Europe laid the groundwork for her career, that is where we started our conversation. Cordelia graduated from Reed College in 1936, having studied languages and literature, primarily German. Soon after, she and a friend journeyed to Grenoble, France, to live with a family and study French. France was in political turmoil, its politicians sparring over domestic labor policies, while, next door, Hitler was rearming Germany. As Cordelia described her host family, they were practically unaware of anything beyond their city's borders. "They had a sublime arrogance about being French," she said. "They had heard of California and Hollywood, but

ILLUS. 3.1   Cordelia Hood as an older woman, circa 2006.
Photograph courtesy of Sarah Fisher.

when I talked about Oregon, they thought it was still the Wild
West—that was all. They had no understanding of the kind of
country the United States was." Even Paris was not of interest;
it was too far, too big, and too foreign. Adolf Hitler was scarcely
a blip in their field of vision.

When I knew Cordelia in her eighties and nineties, she was a confident, accomplished woman. I could not imagine her a shy twenty-something, but that is how she described herself. Hesitant to speak French, she sat quietly at the family's dinner table, listening to the rapid conversation of the *monsieur* and the *madame* and the several children. Finally, one evening, tired of being on the sidelines, she plunged in. "The *monsieur* was so surprised that he blurted out, '*Ma petite barbare, elle parle.*' He actually referred to me as the little barbarian."

The little barbarian apparently needed watching. "I never thought that in my adult life I would be chaperoned at the movies, but I was. There was a very nice Czech boy who was also in the class for foreigners, and he used to walk home with me. That apparently disturbed them, that he would walk home with me. So the next thing I knew, there would be one of them outside the door waiting for me to walk home. And it baffled me entirely, this determination." Finally, the *madame* explained: "You've got to be a virgin before you're married. After you're married, you can do anything you want."

Several months into their stay, Cordelia's friend became engaged to one of the family's sons, and everyone turned their attention to wedding plans—everyone, that is, except Cordelia. She was not about to languish in a remote town, listening to months of discussion about menus and flowers. She would set out on her own, but first, she and the bride-to-be took a final excursion.

In Florence, they visited the parents of a college friend, Emilio Pucci, son of one of the oldest noble families in Florence. Emilio was still in the United States, and before Cordelia left for Europe, he had asked her to take presents to his family. From her modest *pensione,* she called the villa and asked to speak to Emilio's mother. The maid immediately hung up. Baffled, Cordelia asked the proprietor for help. "She wanted to know what I had said, and I said I had asked for Signora Pucci. 'Of course the maid hung up on you. She was right to do so. She is the Marchesa Pucci,' she told me. When she put the call through, the marchesa came on the line, and she was lovely. She invited my friend and me to lunch. It was a lovely luncheon with a lot of young Florentine aristocrats, all of whom spoke perfect English."

Cordelia must have made an impression. Later, the marchesa encouraged Emilio to propose marriage. She liked the idea of fresh American blood invigorating the Florentine aristocratic circle. But by the time Cordelia and Emilio saw each other again, the war had complicated their lives in ways impossible to predict in this prewar idyll.

When her friend returned to Grenoble, Cordelia traveled alone through Italy before venturing to Germany, where she met her brother Daniel, who had been expelled from Reed for driving his car across the campus lawn. Their parents thought a change of environment would be good, so they sent him to be with Cordelia in Europe.

Meanwhile, their sister Lisbeth had been taking acting lessons in New York. When she landed a role that would have her appearing onstage in only a corset, her father decided she, too, would be better off in Europe. The three siblings spent most of a year traveling together.

Lisbeth reminisced with me about the train rides. She was the dreamy one who spent hours looking out the window. Cordelia, the oldest, was the responsible one. While Lisbeth admired the scenery, Cordelia kept her head down, deep in paperwork, tracking their expenses to the penny. When they got to Munich, they found brown-shirted men on every street corner, jutting salutes and chanting heil-Hitlers. Revulsed, they moved on to Austria, thinking it would be safer.

Vienna in winter 1938 was seething with activity. Students from all over Europe packed the universities where Cordelia and Daniel took language classes and Lisbeth studied voice. They joined hundreds, even thousands, of other students who marched in protest of Hitler's proposed Anschluss, carrying the red-and-white Austrian banners. "We went out with them and marched, chanting 'rot weiß rot bis im tod'—'red white red until we're dead.' You know, keep Austria Austrian."

One evening in March, they went to the opera. The famous Vienna State Opera House was constructed in the grand imperial style. Chauffeured cars pulled up to discharge women dressed in long gowns, followed by men in black-and-white dinner clothes. Inside, Cordelia and her siblings climbed to their inexpensive seats in the upper tier. At intermission, they walked through the marble lobby to the loggia that overlooked the Ringstrasse to get some air. "I went out and saw the Viennese police riding around in open cars, as they usually did. But now, all of a sudden, they were wearing swastikas. While we were in the opera, the Germans had come across the border, and they'd all gone Nazi. That really bowled us over, to look down at the ring and see them with swastikas." She realized how naive she had been to think that students chanting in the city's plazas would stop Hitler's advance.

"Later, Lisbeth and I went home, but my silly brother went to a café. He was violent on the subject and almost got his teeth knocked out because he refused to stand up and give a heil Hitler salute."

Quickly, the newly Nazified government closed the universities and began rounding up Jews. Their friend Karl Urbach, an Austrian medical student whose brother Cordelia knew when he had been an exchange student at Reed, urged them to leave the city. Why don't you go skiing, Karl suggested, and he made arrangements for them to stay with a peasant family in the Vorarlberg, near the mountainous border with Switzerland. They could ski and learn the local Swiss German dialect, and he, posing as a casual visitor rather than a fleeing Jew, could cross into Switzerland. But when he tried to do just that, the border guards turned him away. Back in Vienna to apply for exit papers, he was arrested and sent to Dachau.

Word of Karl's abduction reached Cordelia up in the mountains, and she wrote to her father, asking him to use his Washington connections to help, while Karl's family raised money for a bribe. Dachau had not yet become the killing machine it later became, and the money got him freed. With the help of Senator McNarry's office, he obtained a visa and made it to Oregon, where he lived with Cordelia's family and took classes at Reed College. From there, he went to medical school in Chicago and had a long career with the U.S. Public Health Service. As Cordelia spoke to me about Karl, she gestured to a framed photo on the table next to her, and her eyes misted up: he had died only recently.

For the summer, Cordelia and her siblings lived at Lake Attersee in the Austrian Alps with a couple, she a potter, he a violinist and a member of the von Hippel family, a name well known in medicine. With German lessons on the lake, "it was a pretty glorious summer," she said, even though, in the background, Hitler was threatening the Sudetenland and Poland. They hated to leave but could not refuse their parents, who wrote letters, at first asking, then begging them to come home.

Daniel left first and was readmitted to Reed. Lisbeth told me that he later confided in her that Cordelia was the reason he went back to school. Something about the way she combined a rigorous intellect, high expectations, and a genuine interest in other people made him want to perform well.

Cordelia and Lisbeth landed in New York in September 1938, just in time to hear the news that Neville Chamberlain had been to Munich to negotiate an agreement with Hitler. Czechoslovakia would surrender its border region to Germany in exchange for Hitler's pledge of peace. But six weeks later, when Jewish-owned businesses, synagogues, and cemeteries were destroyed in Kristallnacht, the world knew that the Munich Agreement contained only empty words.

Cordelia returned to Reed to complete a master's degree in German, and Lisbeth enrolled at George Washington University. By late 1941, Cordelia, her sister, and her father were in Washington.

In his book *Washington Goes to War,* David Brinkley, then a radio reporter, describes the city: a small southern town suddenly swarmed by thousands who arrived to take war-related jobs, both military and civilian.[2] Social life buzzed with parties and gossip, making it a good place to forge connections and find a job. Cordelia got her first job at the Office of Facts and Figures, where a former Reed professor hired her. Every day, she went to movie theaters to watch the shorts and newsreels that played before feature films, then reported back how the war effort was being presented to the American public.

Within a year, the Office of Facts and Figures merged into the Office of War Information (OWI), and the new agency was given broader responsibility to coordinate and disseminate information. OWI created posters to remind citizens that "loose lips might sink ships." It dropped leaflets on enemy troops designed to undermine their resolve, including messages directly from President Roosevelt in German. To inspire women to fill jobs left vacant by men in the military, OWI had magazines run photographs of women on factory floors. One of the most successful initiatives was Rosie the Riveter, a fictionalized industrial worker based on a real woman. Many images of Rosie became popular, but in Norman Rockwell's iconic rendering, Rosie appears in denim overalls, goggles pushed onto her forehead, cradling a rivet gun on her lap. Her biceps ripple, her red hair is curled, and her lips gleam red.

Cordelia's job had nothing of Rosie's power or glamour, and, after a year spent alone in darkened theaters, she wanted something more exciting. The Pentagon seemed promising. The military was looking for women to fill civilian jobs, and Cordelia had credentials: she was fluent in German and knew something about aviation, from the flying lessons she'd taken as a hobby. She was hired to track deployment of Luftwaffe craft. The Pentagon's huge, five-sided building was new, its parking lot still dirt. When it rained, she trudged to work through a muddy mess.

It was not long before word got around at OSS about the smart, German-speaking woman at the Pentagon. In 1942, OSS was only just getting up and running, and its director, General William ("Wild Bill") Donovan, was hiring, including for the overseas operation.[3]

"I was looking for a way to go overseas," Cordelia recalled. "One is very idealistic at that age. I was very passionate to be sure the Germans were defeated somehow. It seemed I could be more effective overseas. Plus, I wanted to be where the action was. I did not want to spend the rest of the time in the Pentagon, I can assure you."

Excited as she was by the prospect of working for OSS, she had to wait. An interagency no-raid pact was in effect, which meant she had to quit her Pentagon job and be unemployed before OSS could offer her a new job. Then there was another hurdle: she had to go to secretarial school and pass a typing test. "They weren't sending men to secretarial school. That was reserved for girls, I'm afraid."

The idea that women would be typists was pervasive. By the end of the war, nearly forty-five hundred women worked for OSS, nine hundred of them overseas, but only a few were not in the clerical ranks. Cordelia had no way to predict that she would be one of those few, but she was determined to learn to type if it meant going abroad. "Having watched the Germans come into Austria, I felt very strongly about doing what I thought would be effective in defeating Germany," she told me. "My typing was poor, and I couldn't get the hang of the shorthand they were teaching, but they let me have a job anyway. Then they said I would be going to London, which I thought was wonderful."

Nothing in her childhood connected her in any obvious way to the overseas intelligence work that would become her career. That's not the work her parents did, and in any event, no civilian-led intelligence service existed before the war. Yet, seen in retrospect, her childhood contains subtle clues that explain her desire to do this work.

Cordelia was born in 1913 in Portland, Oregon. Her family was of "pioneer stock," as she put it, descended from Daniel Boone. That connection was an early imprint. Both her father and brother were named for him, and among close friends, her father was "Boone." When Cordelia was six, the family moved a few miles into the countryside to what was then the small farming community of Milwaukie. Her mother instigated the move. "She thought we should live outside the city on a polite farm sort of place," Cordelia said. "She thought it would be healthy for us to have chickens and cows and such right there." Most of the neighbors were small farmers who struggled to make a living. In that environment, her family stood out. They lived in a large house up on a hill, surrounded by ten acres of land with an ornamental park, fruit trees, vegetable gardens, coops for chickens and turkeys, and a hired man to help with the gardening.

Before marriage, Cordelia's mother had run a photography studio in Oregon City, but as a wife and mother, she devoted all her time to the family. Cordelia's father worked for a newspaper before he opened a small law office in Milwaukie, where he tried to earn a living on cases the local farmers brought him. Sometimes they paid his fee in vegetables.

The obvious gap in socioeconomic class with their neighbors meant Cordelia and her siblings had to navigate the gulf. "We were set aside because we had this large house up on a hill, and we were not farmers," Cordelia remembered. "At school, the other students came from backgrounds very different from ours. Both my parents had grown up in pioneering families who had moved from the East to the West. The big drive in both my parents, and particularly in my father, was education and reading. We had a very extensive library, and I doubt that my classmates' parents had any library at all. It was an introduction to a very different kind of life."

Cordelia described herself as a quiet child, withdrawn and academic. She admitted that "*academic* is a silly word for a child growing up, but reading was my passion. I'd often run away and hide with a book where nobody could find me." Her one close friend was a girl with whom she took piano lessons.

Lisbeth, three years younger, had a different personality, outgoing and artsy. She was prized on the high school softball team for her skill as a left-handed pitcher, and she liked to travel around the state for games and social events. When their mother called for help with chores, Lisbeth was the first to respond. Sometimes she suggested calling Cordelia to pitch in, but their mother said don't bother: Cordelia was probably reading and wouldn't want to be disturbed. The result of this, Cordelia confided, was that "I did not learn the domestic arts I probably should have learned."

Daniel had a tougher time at school than the girls did. When he got good grades, the other boys laughed at him. When he wore nice clothes, he was picked on. Sometimes he came home from school with ripped clothes and dried blood on his face.

After trying to make a go of it, Cordelia's father gave up his law practice and took a job with the Portland Chamber of Commerce. Construction of the Bonneville Dam, to turn the Columbia River into a source of hydroelectric power, was one of the Chamber's priorities, and that was his assignment. When Senator McNarry took on the issue, he went to Washington as part of the senator's staff.

Despite their different personalities, Cordelia and Lisbeth were close. Together they pored over picture books of Europe and dreamed of travels they might take someday. Richard Halliburton, a well-known travel writer in the 1930s, was a favorite. When Cordelia traveled in Italy as part of her postcollege trip, she followed one of his itineraries. "I'd read everything he had written, and I went to Rome and then Capri because he'd

ILLUS. 3.2 Cordelia Hood as a young woman, undated.
Photograph courtesy of Sarah Fisher.

written about the Blue Grotto there. It was all very romantic."
In music as well, her taste ran to the romantic, including the
composer Robert Schumann, whose pieces she played on the

piano. In college, she had an affinity for romantic German poetry. This inclination toward the romantic, coupled with the family's pioneering heritage and her own taste for adventure, coalesced and underpinned the life she eventually constructed for herself.

Another influential factor was her father's work. From him, she absorbed the idea that government is a force for good, as she saw directly when his behind-the-scenes work helped Karl Urbach to safety. When I knew her many decades later, after her lifetime of experience and travel, she was well aware of American blunders and problems, but she was as patriotic as she had been as a young woman. And when war arrived, it gave her an unprecedented opportunity to work for the country.

In late September 1944 Cordelia and three other women boarded an ocean liner, bound for OSS jobs in Europe. The liner, repurposed for troop transport, was filled with British officers. "Our ship was the *New Amsterdam,* but of course they had blacked out the name," Cordelia said. "Because she was a fast ship, she didn't have to go with an escort, even though there was a lot of submarine activity in the North Atlantic. At night, no light could be showing. You couldn't stand outside and smoke or anything like that. Everything was locked up. Total blackout.

"We went all the way south to keep away from submarines before coming up to England. We were allowed only so much luggage, and since I was going to London for the winter, I brought warm clothes. But it got hotter and hotter as we went south, and I was really uncomfortable."

The three women disembarked in Glasgow, serenaded by the troops, and caught a night train for London. Looking out into the dark, Cordelia caught glimpses of train stations. Each one seemed to have the same name. Peculiar, she thought, that so many villages would be called Marmite. Later she realized that station names had been stripped away to confuse enemy infil-trators, and what was left were the ubiquitous advertisements for England's favorite jamlike spread.

At the London OSS station, she was assigned to X-2, the coun-terintelligence unit, and given the highest security clearance so she could work on the Ultra operation. The German code had been broken in what was one of the most significant intelligence triumphs of the war, and intercepted communiqués were being deciphered, translated, and analyzed. Ultra along with Magic, America's breaking of Japanese ciphers, were cited as major contributions to the Allies' eventual victory.[4]

But before Cordelia could dig in, she had to improve her typing. "In London, they told me to go to secretarial school again, to learn to type better. I was also taught something called speed writing, which I still use. Actually, it's very easy. You just write consonants." I could see the speed writing, there on her pad. As for typing, it was a struggle, but she passed—just barely.

Another OSS employee, Elizabeth McIntosh, later wrote a book about women in the agency, including Cordelia and the more famous Julia Child and Marlene Dietrich. About the counterintelligence unit, she wrote, "Discrimination against women in government service during the war was obvious. The women in X-2, for example, were fully as well educated as the men, they spoke the same number of foreign languages, on average were the same age (early thirties), and most had traveled abroad. But in X-2 they were secretaries, filing clerks, or translators." None was in an executive position.[5]

Yes, there was discrimination, but Cordelia did not use the word when we talked. Instead, she asked if I had read McIntosh's book *Sisterhood of Spies*. It turned out I had, but she wasn't recommending it. From her perspective, denouncing discrimination, though justified, was too easy. It failed to reflect the subtleties of the path she eventually took, in OSS and later. It is also my private speculation that Cordelia did not want to be branded a victim of discrimination. Victimhood did not become her.

Most nights in London, Cordelia worked late, poring over intercepts and pecking out translations on the typewriter. Cold air crept into the office around the blackout curtains that covered the windows and door. When she finally left and picked her way back to the group apartment she shared with other OSS women, she had to contend with the blackout and bombs. "I had to hold the torch pointing down, like this, so no light would show." She demonstrated the angle of the light. "Almost nightly, bombs came down. They came at pretty regular intervals and the alarms would go off. Then there would be an all-clear, and then another alarm. At first, we all tromped down to the basement. Then our landlord asked if we really wanted to do that. It turns out, the

English had just stopped doing it. You couldn't, he said, get any sleep that way. Eventually we stopped too."

Several months into the job, Paul Blum, another OSS employee, landed in London. He was on his way to Bern, Switzerland, where OSS European headquarters were located, but he stayed in London long enough to get to know Cordelia and observe her at work. He did not forget her.

Then, in December 1944, she received an unusual assignment: instructions came from Bern that she was to escort two men to Zurich. They had been in London for a Socialist Party conference and were headed home. Early one morning, a car came for her and the two Swiss men and drove them to an unmarked airstrip in the English countryside, where a small group huddled in the cold: two German prisoners of war who were heading back to Germany with radio transmitters, a dangerous mission that could get them killed; their OSS escorts; and Chuck Yeager, the twenty-one-year-old American fighter pilot whose record for shooting down German planes had already made news, long before he'd broken the sound barrier. They climbed into the C-47, strapped themselves into bucket seats along the sides, and took off over the English Channel.

It was cold, and everyone except Yeager was jumpy. The Battle of the Bulge was under way, and as they flew near the French–Belgian border, fighter planes came close. Cordelia, sitting next to Yeager, observed him studying the action. "His whole focus was on the planes, and when we began to see bursts of antiaircraft fire, then he was really interested." She asked the question everyone was thinking: how much danger are we really in? "Oh, ours is a good pilot," Yeager said in his West Virginian accent. "He's got shrapnel in his belly. That's why he's doing this milk run."

As they approached Lyon, a snowstorm closed in, obscuring bomb craters on the runway. They bumped to a stop. "There was an ambulance waiting because they were afraid the pilot couldn't get in around the bomb craters. But when we landed, everyone waiting for us cheered. Of course, they were excited about Yeager. He was well known by that time."

That night, they repaired to an OSS-run hotel before continuing on their separate journeys. "It was what they called a Joe house, an agent house," Cordelia said. "The next day a car was supposed to come from the consulate in Geneva to pick us up, but it couldn't get through because of the Battle of the Bulge. So there I was with my two Swiss, trying to figure out how we were going to get to Switzerland. Finally I found the OSS driver who came to take the POWs to the German border. He agreed to swing around to the Swiss border first and drop off the three of us. 'But,' he said, 'I have a problem. I don't have a permit to carry this many civilians so you're going to have to pose as my French girlfriend and sit up front with me.' That's fine, I said, as long as I don't have to speak French. With my American accent, no one would believe I was French. The driver also said, 'For God's sake, keep those two Swiss quiet. The Resistance is out looking for Germans. If they say anything, there will be trouble.'"

Everyone in the car practically held their breath, but they made it to the border, a hundred miles away, without running into any patrols. The driver deposited Cordelia and the two men near Geneva. Without any train or bus service, she had to convince the Swiss border guards to call a taxi. She and the two men arrived in Geneva by cab.

"Going into Switzerland was an experience, because the lights were on," she remembered. "In London, everything was blacked out at night. It was definitely strange to see lights all of a sudden. We went into the Buffet de la Gare, where I had a martini. It was the first drink I'd had in ages. In London, a group of us sometimes shared a bottle of sherry, but we had to make it last for a month. Then I had some wine. The Swiss men must have thought I was an alcoholic, I got so tipsy. And we had all these wonderful things to eat. In London, things were pretty restricted. Not much fresh food was coming in. So we had this nice dinner and then I went to Bern to meet Paul Blum."

OSS headquarters was housed in a three-hundred-year-old Swiss burgher's mansion. Allen Dulles, head of European operations, may have noticed its charm, but more to his liking was the fact that it had two entrances: a street door surveilled by German and Swiss agents around the clock and a secluded garden entrance for discreet comings and goings. Dulles had assembled a staff from Americans who were left stranded in Switzerland when the borders closed. For intelligence, he relied on a wide range of sources, including those who were unconventional by

American standards, such as the socialists Cordelia had just accompanied to Switzerland. That assignment, though, was cover for what was really a change of station, requested by Blum and approved by Dulles. She was in Bern for the rest of the war.

Cordelia could not have gotten to Bern much earlier than when she did. Until the latter part of 1944, the Swiss borders were under German control. Only after military operations pushed the Germans back were the Allies able to take control of the borders. Americans like Paul Blum and Cordelia entered Switzerland, and Allen Dulles traveled to France to meet William Donovan, his boss, for their first meeting in nearly two years.

"Paul and I went to work building up our counterintelligence files. The Germans had a big representation in Switzerland at the time. They had stashed their intelligence people in the consulates. Those were the people we were trying to find out about."

The most obvious source for what they wanted to know was the Swiss federal police who monitored the Germans, but they would not share. "The Swiss maintained a rigidly neutral stance, because they were trying to keep the Germans from invading," Cordelia explained. "They were very clear on that score. They did not make any effort to facilitate our information gathering. They were not helpful, not until it became clear that the Germans were losing the war."

Paul knew only a few words of proper German, and none of the Swiss German dialect most of the police officers spoke. Cordelia, however, could manage the dialect, thanks to the winter she spent in the Vorarlberg, and it was her job to convince the police to spill their information. She failed, at first. "When they saw I was a woman, they thought Paul had sent someone low level or tried to pawn off a stenographer on them. They were kind of insulted," she said. "Then Paul suggested we take them to lunch. We'd have a really nice lunch and he'd treat me like an equal, and then they would start to open up. Plus, I could speak their language, which he couldn't."

She cultivated other sources as well. "I was talking to a lot of people—Swiss, Austrians, North Italians. With them I had to prove I knew what I was talking about. I couldn't establish myself as fast as a man could," and here she practically shrugged, "but you just have to get over that male–female thing."

The information began flowing, but typing remained a struggle. Cordelia and Paul spent evenings pecking out memos for Washington. "My job was intelligence analyst, but in that situation, you did everything that came along, whatever was needed. I talked to people, then I had to write dispatches for Washington and get them into the pouch. That kept me there 'til late at night correcting all of my mistakes. It was very educational, but exhausting, because in those days, we had to use carbon paper for our copies."

The Bern station coordinated all kinds of intelligence operations. Gary van Arkel, a labor lawyer from Washington, came to make contact with the underground labor movement in Germany. "The whole idea was to overthrow the Nazis, in any way possible, including through sympathetic labor unions." Tracy Barnes, another lawyer turned OSS operative, came to coordinate with the North Italian partisans. As colorful as these and other colleagues were, however, it took Eileen Sullivan, a real secretary, to impose order. "She was from New York and spoke New Yorkese only. The whole group of us were well integrated and working hard and having a good time. As I said, Switzerland was such a change from England that it was a good life."

The job Cordelia was asked to do—get information, evaluate it in the moment, and confirm or qualify it—sounds amorphous, but she was good at it. Over the years, I had seen her with a range of people—other retired intelligence officers, the man who did her yard work, my young son—and she was comfortable with all of them. She was truly interested in others. That went a long way in her business, where establishing a connection was critical. She also remembered what she heard. Until just a few years before her death at age ninety-eight, she rarely had to look up a phone number. If she had called a number before, she simply remembered it.

By early 1945, an Allied victory began to seem likely, and American intelligence planned for the aftermath, including war crimes trials, which ultimately were held in Nuremberg. For evidence, Dulles wanted to use the diaries of Count Galeazzo Ciano, husband of Edda Mussolini, Benito Mussolini's daughter. The count had served in his father-in-law's government while, at the same time, carefully recording his opposition, hoping to rehabilitate himself in the future, when the fascists fell from power. But before he could deploy the diaries, Mussolini had him executed. The diaries then became the object of a three-way search: the Germans wanted to destroy them; the Americans wanted to safeguard them; and Paul Ghali, a reporter with the *Chicago Daily News,* wanted a big, international scoop. For the widow, they represented financial and political leverage. She knew where her husband had hidden them but couldn't get to them because the Germans had her confined. Nevertheless, she managed to get word to Emilio Pucci, her sometime lover who also happened to be Cordelia's college friend.[6]

Cordelia summarized the intricate plot. "While under house arrest, Edda turned to Emilio for help escaping to Switzerland. She feared for the lives of herself and the children, rightly I think. Emilio was in the Italian air force at this time, but he went AWOL to help Edda. He got her and the children to cross the Alps into Switzerland, with Edda disguised as a peasant woman. Edda was carrying the Ciano diaries. She knew perfectly well that her future livelihood depended on hanging on to those diaries and selling them to the highest bidder."

When Cordelia told Dulles that she and Emilio were college friends, he dispatched her to Zermatt to get Emilio's help with the diaries. The Swiss had stashed Emilio in Zermatt, miles away from Edda, because, as Cordelia explained, they did not want any "hanky-panky." Zermatt, home to the Matterhorn and a ski resort, was hardly a hardship post. "It was fun meeting him again. He was a beautiful skier. He skied in a rather spectac-ular fashion, with his arms widespread. The Swiss called him the Zermatta Engel [Zermatt Angel]. Emilio would come down spectacularly. He was spectacular at everything he did. I was not a good enough skier to keep up with him, but I did my best. One thing we did was enter a dancing contest at the resort one evening, which we won. That was our claim to fame. Meanwhile, I was trying to find out about the diaries. He got a little bitter afterward. He said I came up there not because of our friendship but just to pick his brain."

There was truth in what he said. Cordelia was not simply socializing; she was committed to doing her job. If there ever had been a possibility that Emilio would propose, as the marchesa

ILLUS. 3.3   Cordelia Hood and Emilio Pucci, undated. Photograph courtesy of Sarah Fisher.

once hoped, it had evaporated with the geopolitical realities of the war. Cordelia would live in Europe for many years, not as an American ornament of the Italian aristocracy, but affiliated with an American cause in which she believed.

Ultimately, a deal for the diaries was struck. Edda released them so Dulles could have them photographed for the trials, and the reporter who had searched for them got his scoop. Emilio, meanwhile, was stranded in Switzerland, still AWOL. At Cordelia's suggestion, Dulles arranged a pardon with the Italian Embassy in Switzerland so Emilio could return to Italy without a court-martial. When the war was over, he began the fashion design business that made him famous.

Near the end of the war, Dulles picked up signs that SS general Karl Wolff, commander of German troops in Italy, was contemplating surrender. If true, this would directly contravene Hitler's orders to fight to the death. Also, if true, Dulles was officially required to rebuff any such feeler because the Allies wanted unconditional, not partial, surrender. Also, the Americans knew that Stalin was likely to suspect, or even undermine, any arrangement made without him. But when General Wolff made clandestine contact, Dulles got permission to meet with him. A series of secret messages and covert meetings ensued, followed by unnerving silences. The Americans were left wondering whether any agreement at all could be reached.[7]

While this game of cat and mouse was going on, a woman named Nam de Beaufort surfaced. She had been a professional photographer in Berlin before the war and an early member of the underground opposition to Hitler with multiple colorful roles: mistress of a high-ranking German officer, accomplice to the von Stauffenberg group that attempted to assassinate Hitler, and secretary to German military intelligence in Milan. There she stole documents, including the code book, and passed them to another Resistance member, who got them to Dulles in Bern.[8] When the Germans became suspicious of Nam, the Americans extracted her from Milan and sent Cordelia to meet her. "They sent me down to Zurich to talk to Nam, to try to calm her down and find out whatever information she had to give—what the German Army headquarters in North Italy were up to." Her information smoothed the path to an understanding, and on May 2, 1945, Wolff, together with other key German officers, defied their Fuhrer's order and surrendered close to nine hundred thousand troops. That set the stage for surrender, a week later, of all German forces.[9]

When the war was finally over, Americans wanted no more foreign intelligence operations. They craved domestic stability, not foreign intrigue, and OSS was quickly shut down. But a small segment pushed to continue intelligence gathering, particularly those who foresaw the coming struggle with the Soviet Union. Quietly, certain OSS personnel carried on a skeleton operation, including Cordelia, who remained in Switzerland, probing Soviet networks.

Back in Washington, her father became suspicious. Previously, her government paychecks came to him for deposit. Now, OSS was officially dissolved, and the paychecks were different. "He

ILLUS. 3.4   Cordelia Hood, undated. Photograph by Nam de Beaufort, courtesy of Sarah Fisher.

couldn't figure out why I was getting checks signed by a private citizen," Cordelia said. "That was to conceal my work, but my father got up in arms and started storming around. Through the senator's office, he had ways to find out. He was reassured I was not being kept by some strange man in Switzerland. But there was a series of letters between us, all of which, of course, were being read by the American censor in Switzerland. My father's letters were irate, and I think the censor must have told someone that they needed to calm this man down, otherwise he's going to make trouble."

Events in 1946 bolstered the case that the country needed an intelligence service. Diplomat George Kennan sent his famous "Long Telegram," in which he described the Soviet Union as fearful, truculent, powerful, and out to weaken all rivals. In a commencement address at Westminster College, Winston Churchill warned that an "iron curtain" had fallen across Europe and that Moscow would try to control everything to the east. Mindful of these events, President Truman decided to establish a rudimentary service, eventually to be called the Central Intelligence Agency (CIA).

Cordelia was not, in fact, having an affair with a shadowy man in Switzerland, but she had met someone. Toward the end of the war, Bill Hood arrived in Bern with a military intelligence unit. Seven years younger than Cordelia, he combined intelligence and charm in a way that gave him the panache of someone older. In photographs, he tended to look straight into the camera, as though daring it to capture his secrets. Lisbeth's word for him was "hypnotic."

Cordelia and Bill married in 1950 in Washington, D.C., and honeymooned in New York City, going to jazz clubs every night. Then they returned to Europe, where both were poised to work for the CIA. Within a few years, Cordelia's wartime boss, Allen Dulles, would be the director of central intelligence. They were already friends with Richard Helms and his then-wife Julia, who hosted a party for their wedding, and he would become director in the 1960s. In short, Cordelia and Bill were an espionage power couple.[10]

In Vienna, they lived in a big house on Strudlhofgasse, just around the corner from the American Embassy's magnificent building on Boltzmanngasse. Like Berlin, Vienna was a divided city, with four sectors under Allied control. Geographically close to Soviet-controlled Czechoslovakia and Hungary, yet part of the West, Vienna straddled the two worlds, attracting thousands of refugees, defectors, and spies. As chief of operations, and later chief of the Vienna station, Bill held influential positions in a pivotal location.

Cordelia, on the other hand, was flummoxed. Given the agency's anti-nepotism policy, she could not work on the operational side, which Bill supervised. The alternative, which she took, was to resign and wait for the Office of Policy Coordination (OPC) to come into being. When it did, she returned on a contract basis so that she would be available to move with Bill wherever he was assigned.

OPC handled counterintelligence, using a range of covert actions. It was behind the creation of Radio Free Europe, which broadcast uncensored news to listeners behind the Iron Curtain, and initiated the Congress for Cultural Freedom, which promoted intellectual and cultural life internationally. Operations like those were considered successes, but others were ridiculous. "Somebody in Washington got the bright idea of printing the picture of the Communist Party leaders in Hungary on toilet paper," Cordelia remembered. "They sent us a tremendous carton full of this damn toilet paper. We were supposed to sneak it onto the trains, because the trains were running between Vienna and Budapest. This was supposed to show how disrespectful we were of their leaders. It didn't work. It was impossible. If you bribed some Austrian who was cleaning the train to put the stuff on, they would be discovered, because the moment the train got into Hungary, it would be checked. The CIA station in Vienna ended up with a lot of toilet paper with the pictures of these Communist Hungarian leaders."

One assignment, not ridiculous, was to debrief a defector from Hungary's internal security service. As Cordelia explained, "we Americans knew the Soviets were controlling the security services in Czechoslovakia, Hungary, and Poland, all the satellite states. But we didn't know how much they controlled it. Whether they trained them in place or took them up to Moscow for training, for example. That's what I was to find out. I went up to a CIA safe house in Berchtesgaden, near Salzburg, and spent several weeks talking to this man. I got a briefing on the complete control the Soviets had of the Hungarian service. That's why he had defected, frankly. He was sick and tired of it. They'd

ILLUS. 3.5   Cordelia and Bill Hood, undated. Photograph courtesy of Sarah Fisher.

sent him to Moscow to be trained, and when he came back, the Soviet KGB watched everything he did."

Was he willing to talk? "When I arrived, I could feel him pulling back, because they had sent a woman in. He didn't want to talk to a woman. Once again, I had to establish my bona fides."

How to manage that? "I was working through an interpreter. I had to ask questions, very specific questions, to let him know that I knew what I was talking about. I was a KGB specialist, and eventually I established, in his mind, my right to be there."

The debrief aside, most of Cordelia's work was at a desk. But being married to the chief of station gave her another role, too, which was to look out for the well-being of the agency staff. When I met with one of her friends from the old days, Claire Fieldhouse told me about the evening she and her fiancé Jack went to the Hoods' house in Vienna to announce their engagement. Bill, as Jack's boss, had to approve the marriage for security purposes, and he did, spending nearly twenty minutes assuring Jack that marriage to Claire was perfectly compatible with the work he would be asked to do. Meanwhile, Cordelia took Claire aside for a private talk.

"What do your parents think of the match?"

"They're happy for me," Claire said. "But in truth, they don't know much about Jack."

"Have they met him?"

"No, not yet. I did write them a letter."

"What did you tell them in your letter?"

Not much, Claire confessed, and Cordelia thought they should hear more. She wrote to them herself, emphasizing what she thought was important—Jack's military service and his career prospects. Then, Cordelia helped Claire plan the wedding, and when children came along, she became a devoted surrogate aunt.

Cordelia and Bill had no children of their own. Children, she told me, would have kept Bill from buying the succession of Jaguar cars he so much enjoyed. I heard regret in her words, and lingering bitterness from the divorce. But as long as they were married, they were close to their nieces and nephews. Sarah, one of Lisbeth's daughters, spent a year with them in Frankfort, where they were stationed in the 1960s. Bill introduced her to photography and jazz, his favorite hobbies. On weekends, Cordelia and Bill, with Sarah in the Jaguar's rumble seat, drove through the countryside. They thought nothing of traveling an hour or two to a fine restaurant. At home Cordelia was the cook, and Sarah watched her aunt in the kitchen. She approached a recipe analytically, never deviating. A quiche was assembled in the prescribed order, bacon spread on the crust before the eggs were added. She was, Sarah said, an "intellectual cook."

The overseas stations where Cordelia and Bill were posted—Vienna, Frankfurt, Munich, Bern—were tight-knit communities of Americans closely bound by oaths of confidentiality, and the same oath applied when they were on home duty in Washington. Coworkers spent many evenings together, at diplomatic receptions or at one another's homes. Often, the private dinners ended with the men holed up in intense discussion of ongoing operations and the women chatting casually in a separate room. Cordelia would have felt torn. With her experience in the field, she was as able as any man to converse about operations, but she could not desert the women.[11]

My husband remembers the aftermath of one dinner in particular. He was a young teenager, with his parents at the Hoods' house in Washington for the evening. When dinner was over, Bill rose and said the guests would have to excuse his wife for the remainder of the evening—she was going upstairs to pack his suitcase because he was leaving the next day for an assignment.

The end of the marriage, when it came, was difficult. Bill was ready for a new relationship, and Cordelia took a financial hit. "I was working in the field from 1943 to approximately 1980, except for when I had to retire," she said. "Then I came back and did contract work. I'd always work when we were in Washington. I took a beating in grade raises, because of being on contract. When I retired, I didn't have as high a retirement pay as if I had worked straight through. I was on contract because I was married to Hood."

Reflecting on the impact that marriage had on her career, Cordelia confided that she and Bill never seriously discussed whose career would take precedence. They just assumed it would be his. The rule against nepotism may have had a benign goal, but it ended up having an adverse effect on women, given the assumption about whose career really counted. As things turned out, Bill did indeed enjoy a full, successful career of thirty years, retiring as executive officer of the counterintelligence staff, a position only several steps removed from the directorship itself.

Yes, there was bitterness after the divorce, partly because of money and probably heightened by Bill's subsequent remarriage. Later, they did get past some of it, and they retained a mutual respect. When I called Bill to confirm some details of this account, he assured me, "You can rely on whatever Cordelia says."

Yet, even if Cordelia and Bill had talked frankly about what each wanted for a career, it is doubtful she would have had anything close to the opportunity he did. Statistics about women working inside the CIA are hard to find, but when I made a Freedom of Information Act request, an interesting document turned up. In the agency's first decade, every one of its employees at the executive level was male, and nearly the same was true for the grade levels below executive. Only in the lowest ranks were women a significant presence.[12]

None of this is surprising. CIA officer ranks were full of men who were qualified by virtue of having worked for OSS or military intelligence during the war, where they never encountered women in supervisory positions. They were used to male colleagues and not at all accustomed to women in positions equivalent to theirs. A woman, even one as talented and committed to the work as Cordelia, simply did not fit the prevailing image of who belonged at the highest levels of the CIA. Not until seventy years after the agency was established did a woman serve as its director.

Gender-based assumptions were hardly limited to the intelligence field. For jobs of all types, newspaper help-wanted ads specified requirements for both age and gender. For example, in the "female help wanted" section of the Boston Globe in 1944, Chelsea Clock advertised for a personnel assistant between the ages of twenty-five and thirty-five. Middlesex Button Company wanted "girls" from "eighteen to thirty-five." Farrington Manufacturing sought "Girls and Women" aged "sixteen to fifty."

When men were scarce, as they were during the war, employers targeted women. Western Union, for instance, recruited women for positions "vital to war work." Cambridge Rubber looked for women to make parkas and ponchos for the navy. Walter Baker, the chocolate company, wanted women to produce chocolate for "men and women in the Armed Forces." As the Baker ad bluntly stated, women hired to make chocolate would do "jobs formerly done by men and will be required to work on all shifts."[13]

Women joined the labor force in droves, often in the manufacturing sector, but even in professional fields, new opportunities

ILLUS. 3.6 At dinner with my mother-in-law, Ilse Grainger; my husband, Andrew Grainger; and Cordelia Hood, circa 2002. Photograph courtesy of our son James Stone.

opened because of the war. For instance, law firms, faced with a shortage of male lawyers, allowed women lawyers to step away from their secretarial desks and handle clients' cases. Medical schools relaxed quotas, and some even became co-ed. Harvard's medical school, which had been exclusively male for two hundred years, debated whether it should admit women to fill the empty seats. Author Mary Roth Walsh describes the 1943 meeting where the faculty took up the issue. There were, she says, "scenes of disorder and confusion," but in the end, a majority voted to admit "very superior women" instead of "mediocre men."[14]

I envision the war as a sort of fulcrum, the point where everything balanced. Like a seesaw inclined in one direction, the culture tipped in favor of women's work opportunities because of the exigent circumstances. OSS, for example, needed someone like Cordelia, who was smart, personable, and fluent in an essential dialect. If the seesaw had continued tipping in that direction, we can only imagine what postwar opportunities might have arisen: equal pay for equal work, a policy the government encouraged during the war, could have been expanded; graduate schools could have eliminated quotas for women; employers could have cast a wide net to hire the best candidates, no matter their gender. But this is not what happened.

Men came home from the war, ready to fill classroom seats and resume the jobs they had left behind. In doctoral, medical, and law programs, the number of women reverted to prewar levels. Then, they dipped further. Most of the women lawyers who had been plucked from secretarial jobs during the war remained associates; only a few advanced to the partner level. The seesaw tipped away from opportunities for women outside the home.

Katharine Graham, publisher of the *Washington Post,* born in 1917, was a contemporary of the women in this book. As she wrote in her autobiography, "we had been brought up to believe that our roles were to be wives and mothers, educated to think that we were put on earth to make men happy and comfortable and to do the same for our children."[15]

Small wonder, then, that there was so little criticism when Adlai Stevenson gave the Smith College commencement address in 1955. The speech has been criticized many times, but it is nonetheless remarkable. Stevenson, former Illinois governor and Democratic presidential candidate, spoke about the future of American democracy. He worried that the traditional values of freedom, tolerance, charity, and free inquiry were at risk. Men had become so specialized in their work that they no longer honed the habits of mind necessary to support such values. But Smith's "gallant girls," as he called them, were in a position to help. You are about to step into the humble role of housewife, he told the graduates. Whether "in the living room with a baby on your lap or in the kitchen with a can opener in your hands," you can keep your man's culture alive. And don't worry about the degree you are about to receive. You can use it to keep your man "straight on the differences between Botticelli and Chianti."[16]

Imagine the social media outrage if that speech were made today. Even in 1955, I thought there might have been complaints, but I did not find any when I searched the Smith alumnae magazine online. Grumbling, if there was any, was kept out of sight. The seesaw had tipped so dramatically away from women's professional opportunities that Stevenson's worldview was not even questioned. And many women agreed with it.

Intermezzo

After Dinner

The after-dinner dilemma that Cordelia faced, whether to stay with the men or go with the women, was not hers alone. I remember it too.

One evening, when I was in sixth grade, my family had dinner at someone else's house, more than ten of us seated at a long table. At the end of dinner, the women stood up and headed into the kitchen, dirty dishes in hand. The men stayed seated. This was not surprising. I had been at enough group dinners with my family to know what was likely to happen: the men would launch into a conversation about politics and current events, and the women would wash dishes. At our house, things were different. My mother cooked, we kids cleared the table, and my father washed the dishes, with our help. But when we were guests, we deferred to the hosts, and my father stayed at the table with the other men.

That night, I helped clear the table, but inside the kitchen, I stood off to the side, trying to figure out how many women could really fit around the sink. Maybe I wasn't needed? I hoped that was the answer, because I liked discussions about current events. We had them every night at home. My parents talked about what was in the news, and they asked us kids what we thought. If they used a word we didn't know, we sometimes hesitated to ask about it, because we knew what we'd be told—look it up, and let us know what you find.

In the kitchen, my mother noticed that I seemed uncomfortable, shifting from one foot to the other. She knew exactly what I was thinking. When she nodded, I took it to mean, yes, you can go back to the dining room. It was OK by her if a girl was part of the conversation, even if everyone else at the table was a man.

It's strange that I remember something as subtle as my mother's nod. Indirection was not my parents' principal strategy for child-rearing. As I was growing up, they said directly, millions of times, what they expected, what I should and should not do. Yet her quiet nod let me know that she understood the kind of girl I was and who I might grow up to be.

4

Peace and Polio
Martha Lipson Lepow, Physician
(b. 1927)

When I was very young, my mother kept me in the backyard for an entire summer. She allowed me to play with two girls who lived next door, but nothing more. Polio was spreading, as often happened in the summer, and a boy on our street who had been sick now wore metal braces on his legs. My mother was taking no chances.

The year before, we had joined the town's beach association. For a nominal fee, we swam at Morses Pond, where the water, as I remember it, was tepid. I loved spending the day at the pond, eating snacks brought from home, splashing in the shallow water, and ducking under the dock to see the tiny fish that hid there. I wanted nothing more than to spend another summer like that, but it was out of the question. The membership tag hung from a hook in the kitchen, a small metal disc on a rubbery band that slipped over the wrist. The sight of the tag teased me with the memory of a summer that polio made impossible. While I dreamt of swimming, Martha Lipson and others were learning everything they could about how to rid us all of the disease.

Martha worked in Cleveland in what was called the "virus lab," an epicenter of polio research. During the week, she analyzed patient samples for evidence of polio infection and antibodies. On weekends, in the basement of City Hospital, where the lab was cheek-by-jowl with the autopsy facility, she fed monkeys. "I'd throw pieces of Wonder Bread and oranges through a little opening in the cage, where they couldn't reach my fingers. Otherwise, I'd get bitten. It was hot down there, with no air conditioning." Martha was two years out of medical school when she began a specially arranged residency in the lab. It was an entirely unplanned step for Martha, but it turned out to be pivotal both to her career and to her personal life.

I learned about Martha from the alumni office at Oberlin College, my alma mater. I wrote to her at the Albany Medical Center where she worked and asked to meet her. I didn't hear back right away. Then, one Sunday morning, my phone rang. It was Martha. "Let's talk now," she said. "I'm not making rounds this morning. This afternoon I have a rehearsal with my chamber group, but I have time right now."

I was flustered, my standard interview outline filed away. I juggled the phone with one hand and scrambled to find paper and pen. Then I tried to focus on the questions I wanted to ask. As I collected my thoughts, Martha apologized for not having responded sooner, but her schedule had been busy. For three days of the week before, she'd seen patients. Then she'd traveled to Cleveland to attend an endowed lecture in honor of her deceased husband, returning home in time to catch two performances at the Saratoga Performing Arts Center: a matinee of the New York City Ballet, where she joined former colleagues from the University of Connecticut medical school, and an evening performance of Gilbert and Sullivan's operetta *Trial by Jury*. The next night, she'd seen *Cabaret* at the Park Playhouse in Albany. At eighty-six, she was regarded as one of the nation's foremost authorities on childhood infectious disease.

During our call, I wrote notes as quickly as I could, and did so again when we had a second, long phone conversation. Only after Martha cut back on her work schedule, at least a little, did we finally meet.

She was born in Cleveland, Ohio, in 1927. The factories produced steel, auto parts, electrical equipment, and instruments and drew both native-born and foreign-born workers to the jobs. By 1950, Cleveland was the fifth largest city in the country. For an aspiring doctor, its infrastructure of hospitals and universities was fertile ground.

Both sides of Martha's family included recent immigrants. Her maternal grandparents had come from Poland, her father and his family from Russia. Her father's family had emigrated in stages. His six older sisters left first, urged by their father, who knew he was powerless to protect them from pogroms and the Cossacks who targeted young women. In Cleveland, the sisters rented market stalls where they sold local produce and, later, opened their own small grocery stores. By the early 1900s, they were able to bring over the rest of the family. According to Martha, her aunts were "smart, street-wise, and strong-willed." They had no question that their younger brother, Martha's father, should be educated, and they pooled their grocery store earnings to help with his tuition.

Martha's parents met in college, at Flora Stone Mather College for Women and Adelpert College, the two single-sex institutions that later became part of Case Western Reserve University. He was headed to medical school, she to business school in New York, where women learned stenography and typing, a curriculum nothing like that of today's business schools. Back in Cleveland they married, had Martha, and, six years later, welcomed her younger sister Natalie.

Growing up, Martha saw much of her extended family. Though she was only one of thirty cousins, the six aunts managed to keep tabs on her. When they said "So nu?" Martha knew what they meant—was she dating someone, and was he Jewish? Her parents were relaxed about religion—they had married in a Reform temple and took the girls to shul only on the high holidays—but others in the family felt strongly. Martha's grandmother was so adamant that two of her sons remained bachelors until she died rather than let her know they had gentile girlfriends.

Martha attended Cleveland public schools, and "they were excellent," she said. "Not only were the schools themselves good, but the families whose children walked through the doors had high expectations." She compared her urban high school to its suburban rival. "Even though people in Shaker Heights had a lot of money, Cleveland Heights High School was just as good."

Like many of the families described in this book, hers believed education was key to the future. For them, it was a shared endeavor. As her aunts helped her father, the extended family would help her, and she, in turn, would help her grandchildren. Several times in our conversations, she returned to the subject of education and what it had done for her.

The war was the backdrop to her time in high school—Pearl Harbor in her sophomore year, the Normandy invasion ten days before graduation. In between, she and her friends practiced civil defense drills and rolled bandages with the Junior Red Cross. But day to day, she was busy with classes, field hockey, basketball, singing alto in the school chorus, and dancing the jitterbug.

When she was fourteen, Martha began a long affiliation with a summer camp in Cascade, Maryland, first as a camper, then as a counselor-in-training, a full-fledged counselor, and finally, during medical school, assistant doctor. As a counselor, she oversaw the swim and music programs and played the latest Broadway show tunes for camp sing-a-longs. Her mother had started her on piano when she was three. She was talented, so much so that she and her mother thought music might be her career. But other influences came into play. "Miss Ida, the camp director, was a visionary leader, and Miss Sara, the head counselor, had a feel for working with adolescents and was a real advocate for them."

With women like these in mind, plus her own babysitting jobs at home, Martha began to think she wanted to work with children and adolescents. Drawn as well to science classes at school, she decided nursing would be good. When she told her father what she was thinking, he was blunt.

"No," he said. "You really should do more. You have the ability for medical school."

"You really think so?"

"Yes, I do. You're bright and you have talent in the sciences. And as a doctor, you can be in charge."

This was more than simple encouragement; he was helping her see beyond the popular idea that men were doctors and women were nurses. As Martha told another interviewer, "I had taken on what the prevailing thoughts were, that nice girls don't do real well in math. Whether they could do well in math or not doesn't matter . . . that just seemed to be where society was at that time."[1]

She already had an idea of what a career in medicine involved. Like Muriel Petioni, she had seen her father at work; sometimes she went with him on house calls. Not everyone could afford to pay a doctor, and when one patient gave her father a glass-fronted bookcase as payment for medical services, she understood that.

When she was ten, her father went for more training in neuro-psychiatry, and she became familiar with the hospital setting. "Some nights, when my father was on call, my mother would take my sister and me to eat dinner at the hospital. That was the only way we would get to see him, on one of his breaks."

As she got older, he talked to her about his work. "We would be driving in the car," Martha remembered, "and he would point out a stranger as we passed. He would say, 'See that man? See how he's walking funny? He had syphilis.' Or maybe he'd say it was a stroke. Or something else. Then he'd explain why he thought so, usually an unsteady gait or a withered leg."

Her father's practice was never lucrative, and his return to school, with the Depression still on, meant a gap in the family's income. To close it, her mother took a job in a state social service office, which also made her a powerful role model for Martha. "My mother was ahead of her time in working. I saw her work throughout much of my childhood, as did some of her friends, and that was hugely influential, to see that a woman would work outside the home and still have a husband and children." Martha's words echoed Dahlov Ipcar's, that her mother, too, showed what was possible.

Martha herself got a part-time job in a pharmacy owned by two of her uncles. "I was a Depression baby," she said. "I was born two years before the stock market crash, and I grew up aware of the hard times around me. I understood that having a job was important." Usually, she worked the cash register, except when a customer wanted to buy cigarettes. Being only fifteen, she had to call one of her uncles to ring up the tobacco sale.

For college, Oberlin was a logical choice. It was close to home, only thirty-five miles away. Its history, as the country's first co-ed college and the first to admit students regardless of color, appealed to her. Also, music was everywhere. She had given up the idea that she might be a professional musician. "I wasn't good enough for a performance career, and I didn't think I wanted to teach piano." But music remained a powerful draw. Both a college and a conservatory were on campus, and a student could barely walk from one end to the other without hearing music from somewhere—a practice room, a recital hall, or Finney Memorial Chapel. Martha took organ and harpsichord lessons, but her real focus were the pre-med classes, where she excelled and, as a senior, was a teaching assistant.

"Oberlin helped me," she said. "There was a whole environment that inspired me. The people who went there were wanting to move on. They were socially conscious. And there were no fraternities or sororities. We had those at Cleveland Heights High School, and this was more egalitarian."

When her advisor encouraged her to apply to medical school, he also cautioned her. "You will do well with patients," she remembered him saying, "but medical schools admit only a handful of women each year. Why don't you take a look at Western Reserve? They're making changes."

Western Reserve was indeed overhauling its program, and Dr. John Caughey was a principal player. As dean, he interviewed applicants and ran his list by the admissions committee, and that was pretty much the class. He cast a wide net, including older students, women, racial minorities, even those with nonscience backgrounds. This was an innovative approach in 1948. "Dr. Caughey was legendary," Martha told me. "He was greatly respected, revered really. He was looking for diversity. In my class, there was one Black student, the first one admitted in many years. Cultural sensitivity is today's buzzword, but Western Reserve was thinking about it back then. Cleveland had a mixture of patients, a lot of immigrants, so it was a good place to be teaching students how to treat patients from a real variety of cultures. Dr. Caughey and Western Reserve were very much in the vanguard."[2]

When he interviewed Martha, he tried to test her resolve. "Being a doctor is a tough life," he said, "very demanding. Why do you want to join this rat race?"

She knew why. "I want to learn. I want to learn how to take care of sick people. And mostly, I want to learn about prevention, particularly for children."

Here, another family influence may have come into play. Martha's sister Natalie was quite ill as a child, with effects that lingered into adulthood. Martha got a graphic lesson in how a sick child can affect a family, and it guided her approach throughout her career.

When Martha began medical school, the number of women studying medicine was in flux. Fifteen years earlier, when Muriel Petioni applied, women were about 5 percent of all students. During the war, women's share increased to 10 percent, where it remained for a few years as women finished the programs they had started. By the early 1950s, the percentage had returned to prewar levels and then sunk even lower.[3]

In her class of eighty-seven students were seven women. The school had no women's restrooms or quarters for women on call to sleep, except in the nurses' dorm. Occasionally, a guy told a locker room joke. A few professors in clinical specialties, surgery in particular, were skeptical of women's abilities. And some nurses were "snooty" about women doctors, Martha recalled. But to Martha, these were minor glitches, far outweighed by her excitement in what she was learning. Penicillin, a game changer in treatment, had just become commercially available. Viruses like polio, which, for generations, had killed or crippled patients, were being studied intensely. Scientists were coming to understand DNA's double helix structure. She was a resident when "we had, suddenly in 1953, the description of DNA."[4]

In her last summer of medical school, Martha went back to camp as assistant doctor. On one particular day, an eight-year-old girl came into the infirmary with fever, headache and muscle pain. It just so happened that her father was visiting and the head doctor was away. Martha's first thought was polio. In a previous summer, the camp had closed because of infected campers, and this summer, there were numerous cases in the surrounding area. In a reprise of the many times her father had shared his diagnostic expertise, she asked him to help examine the girl. This time, the patient was in front of them instead of on the sidewalk.

They found no muscle weakness in the girl and concluded that it was a different virus.[5] Nonetheless, she was wise to be vigilant about polio. Every year, the disease left more than fifteen thousand Americans paralyzed.[6] In the year Martha graduated from medical school, 1952, the country recorded more than fifty-seven thousand polio cases and three thousand deaths.[7]

When Martha interned in pediatrics, childhood diseases like measles, chicken pox, meningitis, whooping cough, and scarlet fever were common, sometimes so severe that patients died before their teens. Pediatric intensive care units barely existed. Polio was prevalent among children and adolescents, and Martha cared for many of them at City Hospital. "Their minds were fine," she told me, "but their bodies were sometimes so damaged that they could not swallow on their own and needed tubes in their trachea." Others had trouble breathing and were placed in iron lung respirators. Lined up against the wall, "they looked like large metal coffins, except the patient's head stuck out of the machine. It was surreal to see a ward full of them."[8]

If a polio patient were lucky enough to be released from the hospital, Martha would help the family learn to care for the child. In a chapter she later contributed to a book about polio, she remembered one patient in particular. "I'll never forget Kathy.

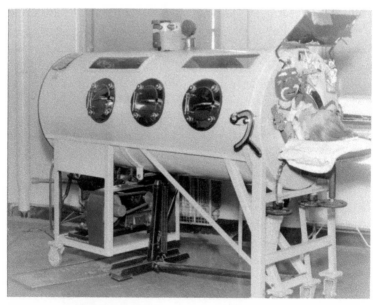

ILLUS. 4.1   Polio patient in an iron lung, undated. Photograph courtesy of Boston Children's Hospital Archives Program.

She eventually went home with her respirator as did many others. All these patients had to have auxiliary power at home in the event of outages. Kathy learned what is called frog breathing which enabled her to survive for short periods if the respirator was opened for care; this technique could have been life saving if the respirator failed. After her discharge, if Kathy had a cold, she would usually have to come back to the hospital because of secretions and poor cough. Sadly, she died of influenza with pneumonia a few years later."[9]

Martha was lucky to work closely with several senior doctors, one of them Dr. Robert Eiben, whom she met when she was an intern. "He was an extraordinarily compassionate, caring physician," she said. "I don't think you'd ever meet a kinder person. As a doctor, he treated the whole person, and he dealt with the patient's family, too, as they all came to terms with the medical problem. He became one of my mentors."

Martha continued in pediatrics as resident, then chief resident, until a routine chest X-ray showed a spot of tuberculosis on her lung. That sent her into isolation, away from patients and most everyone else, for six months. When she felt better, she was itching to get back to work, but her doctor would not allow it: she was still too weak to resume a resident's punishing schedule. Just as she was wondering what to do, Dr. Frederick Robbins, director of the virus lab, paid her a visit. He had previously earmarked her to be chief resident, and she had sent patient samples to his lab for analysis when she worked on the ward. But she never expected he would invite her to work in the lab. When he did, she was not sure she should accept.

According to a Columbia University study, a foremost characteristic of highly educated women is their early commitment to a career path. Once committed, they follow up with conscious and deliberate steps to realize their goals.[10] That describes Martha. She had decided on a career as a teenager. By the time Dr. Robbins offered this position, she had completed ten years of pre-med and medical study on her way to being a pediatrician. The lab would be a step away from patient care and toward research. But, after six months of convalescent reading and listening to music, she was more than ready to do something. She said yes, and the decision changed her life.

The lab was in the vanguard of virology research. Its doctors and technicians were using a novel technique to grow polio virus in tissue culture, rather than in live animals. Dr. Robbins and two colleagues had developed the technique at Children's Hospital in Boston, and it was a critical step in meeting the unprecedented demand for virus that clinical trials of the Salk vaccine created. More than a million children in the United States, Canada, and Finland were to be injected with inactivated polio virus and tested for an antibody reaction. To grow enough virus in live animals would be unwieldy and difficult, whereas growing it in tissue culture was manageable. Once the trials got under way, Cleveland's lab was a designated facility for testing samples.

One morning in October 1954, a lab employee burst through the door with news. That year's winners of the Nobel Prize had just been announced, and Dr. Robbins was one. He and his Boston colleagues were to share the prize for developing the lab's method of cultivating virus. When Dr. Robbins arrived a little later that morning, everyone was buzzing with excitement. He thanked them, then said, "This is just a normal day. We'll get to work now." He was humble, but the prize did mean something, a great deal. As Martha told me, "I would characterize the work in the lab as one of the biggest advances in medicine in the second half of the twentieth century, up there with the development of penicillin."

The antibodies that everyone was hoping to see were indeed present, and on April 12, 1955, the Salk vaccine was declared a success. The next day, a mother from Nyack, New York, wrote to Dr. Salk. Her letter spoke for millions of Americans.

> Dear Doctor Salk—
>
> Not the least among the many honors a grateful world bestows upon you are the blessings of a million mothers to whom your discovery means freedom from a most tragic fear. When I realize that my young daughter and another child as yet unborn will never suffer from polio, I am more grateful than words can express to you and to all the others who have made this possible.
>
> Most sincerely,
> Joanna H. Shurbet[11]

Six years later, the Sabin vaccine was also declared effective, and by the early 1960s, the United States was down to fewer than a thousand new cases. Martha recognized that her bout with TB had presented her with an opportunity and that she was wise to have accepted it. "It was exciting," she said. "I was participating in a preventive effort. This was really the beginning of prevention of infectious diseases, and I was hooked."

The lab also gave her credentials and connections. "I learned to write papers from Dr. Robbins because we had all these specimens in the lab and it was important to write about our work. Having worked with him allowed me to grow academically and to get places I otherwise would not have. I landed well, partly because of that background. He encouraged me to do the work. It made no difference to him that I was a woman."

One place Dr. Robbins wanted Martha to land was a fellowship at Children's Hospital in Boston. He had started a department of adolescent medicine at the hospital, in addition to participating in Nobel Prize–winning work in the lab, and he thought it was a good opportunity for his protégé. Martha agreed. Ever since she was a camp counselor, she had liked working with this age group, and she understood this was a new medical specialty worth pursuing. "Dr. Robbins, he was a visionary. This was very forward looking at the time. He was very encouraging to a younger doctor like me."

On the fellowship, she would work with Dr. John Enders, one of the corecipients of the Nobel Prize. But before she left, Dr. Robbins asked her to help a medical student, Irwin Lepow, learn about tissue culture. Lee, as he was known, already had a PhD, was teaching while getting his MD, and wanted to understand what went on in the lab. Martha gave him an overview, and they continued talking over coffee in the hospital cafeteria. The conversation quickly turned personal. Two months later, they were married.

Martha's aunts were relieved. Finally, "So nu?" brought the answer they wanted to hear. Their niece, the last of the thirty cousins, would be married, and yes, he was Jewish.

Martha's father had other questions. "What are your career plans?" he asked his prospective son-in-law.

"I'm interested in basic science. I'd like to do research in that area."

"You'll be dependent on grants, won't you?"

"Yes, to some extent."

"Well, you'll never make a buck that way."

"I disagree with you, sir," Lee said.

The polite "sir" helped. So did the couple's confidence. "We just thought the marriage would work," Martha said. "We both planned to work, and we would have two incomes."

In theory, Martha could have gone to Boston, even as a newlywed. But, all of a sudden, she had a family—not only a husband but his seven-year-old daughter, Lee's first wife having died of multiple sclerosis. Instead, she sent a letter. "Dear Dr. Enders," she wrote, "I have fallen in love and will not be coming to Boston in July."[12]

When I met Martha in Albany, we had dinner in the senior apartment complex where she lived. After dinner, we went upstairs to her apartment. She turned on the lights, and I spied a glass-fronted bookcase. It was a lovely piece of furniture, the one her father's patient had given him during the Depression. For years, Martha had used it to store dishes in her kitchen. Now that she had downsized into an apartment, it held books and, on top, a row of framed family photos. One particular photo caught my eye. "Oh, yes," she said. "That was taken when we got married. My dress was emerald green, with a black belt. Lee's suit was very dark, nearly black. And Laurie's dress was pale blue. It was the first store-bought dress she ever had." She saw the black-and-white photo in vivid color in her memory.

Martha was delighted to stay in Cleveland, even though it meant giving up the fellowship in Boston. She would have the chance to develop a bond with Laurie, who, she told me, is now her best friend. She also wanted to add to the family, which she soon did by giving birth to two boys. And Cleveland offered excellent professional opportunities. She would have a fellowship in pediatric infectious disease, be on the faculty at Case Western Reserve, and teach at Metropolitan General Hospital, successor to City Hospital, where she was already well known. As she later wrote, "I was committed to an academic career in

ILLUS. 4.2   Martha, Lee, and Lauren Lepow, 1958. Photograph
courtesy of Martha Lepow.

a very rich environment. I would be a clinician, teacher and
investigator."[13]

Inevitably, she and Lee faced the problems, adjustments, and
compromises of working parents everywhere. Fatiguingly familiar today, they were rare in the 1950s, not really part of the public
discourse because women were simply presumed to be the ones
who would handle the home front. But Martha's family did not
fit in that box. She and Lee had to find their own way, since she
was not going to stop working.

One adjustment she made was to give up overnight travel
when the children were young, even though that meant bypass-
ing many of the conferences and lectures by which doctors
become known to the national medical community. She and
Lee worked out a schedule to cover early-morning and evening
hours and used a rotating cast of babysitters, including young
doctors and their spouses. But not until they hired Gussy Walker

did they get the stability and reliability they needed. Gussy was a Black woman, born in rural Alabama, in peanut-growing country. Growing up in the Jim Crow South, she had received no more than a few years of elementary school education. In Cleveland, she lived with her son and husband, who worked at the Swift meat packing plant. Her job with the Lepow family was not unusual. For nonwhite women, private household work was the biggest job category in 1960, just as it was when Ella Madison had worked for Dahlov Ipcar's family some forty years earlier.[14] Given Gussy's limited education, she had few other options.

Even though Martha cut back on some extracurricular activities, she did plenty. Her résumé lists no fewer than eighty articles, thirty book chapters, twenty-eight abstracts, and seven book reviews where she is sole author or coauthor. At Western Reserve, she advanced to assistant professor. She also managed to accept a special fellowship in public health at the University of Oxford in England. At home, she and Lee talked medicine, "probably more than the children wanted to hear."

In 1967, life changed for everyone in the family when the University of Connecticut recruited Lee to head the pathology department at its new medical school. The job offer meant they had to sort out what Martha would do and who would care for the children. The move became feasible, however, when the medical school asked Martha to be acting head of pediatrics and Gussy agreed to move with the family. She was a widow by that time, and her son could finish his last year of high school living with a friend's family, the Lepows covering the additional expenses.

In West Hartford, where they lived, they divvied up the day, with Martha taking her son to swim practice at five in the morning (swimming was her exercise too), Lee holding down the fort at home, and Gussy taking responsibility for after-school hours, driving the kids to afternoon sports practice and their friends' houses. She had never driven before, but she went to driving school and got her first license in Connecticut.

At the medical school, Martha found challenges. The staffing was only beginning to jell, and in her interim position, she lacked the authority of a department head. As an administrator, she was away from what she knew best—patient care and cutting-edge research. The closest she came was setting up a virology lab based on Cleveland's model. "It was the worst two years of my life," she told me. "I didn't really like management. Plus, I was underpaid. My salary was pegged to the salary I had left in Cleveland and that, in turn, was lower than it would have been for a man. The thinking was that a man, particularly a married one, deserved a higher salary than a single woman, or the second wage earner."

The salary inequity was not surprising. The practice of paying a man more had nothing to do with qualifications or perfor-mance; it was an explicit form of social engineering based on widely accepted views of proper roles for men and women. Still, Martha was disillusioned to realize that for all the lab's exciting work and mentoring, its salary policies adversely affected her. She reminded me that "the issue of women being underpaid is always there. If women are not careful, they start out lower and that follows them the rest of their careers. It's hard to make a big jump in salary."

When a permanent department chair was hired, Martha was happy to return to patients and teaching, although she did note that the person hired was a man and that he was paid more than she was. Nonetheless, she became a full professor and was instrumental in bringing medical care to residents in poor sections of Hartford. Having worked in Cleveland with patients from a variety of countries and cultures, she was fully prepared to treat Puerto Rican migrant workers who labored in tobacco fields along the Connecticut River and children exposed to lead paint in their families' run-down apartments. Using some of the research protocols she had learned in the virus lab, she studied the effects of leaded gasoline and testified before Congress in the run-up to passage of the Clean Air Act. She made friends with other doctors and nurses and had stimulating work. "I moved for my husband," she said. Her tone sounded jocular but rueful. I asked her if there was ever tension between them, knowing full well that every couple has some. "Sometimes," she said, "we both could be stubborn."

Rueful or not, she would again move for her husband. Eleven years after they went to Connecticut, Lee got another job offer, this time in Rensselaer, New York, as president of the Sterling-Winthrop Research Institute. This move was easier. The children were out of high school, and Gussy had gone to work

ILLUS. 4.3 Martha and Lee Lepow, circa 1984. Photograph courtesy of Martha Lepow.

for another family. Martha would be a professor and clinical program director at Albany Medical College, a well-established institution. But before that, twenty years after she wrote to Dr. Enders to say she had fallen in love, she went to Children's Hospital in Boston. No longer a young doctor on a fellowship, she was, at age fifty-one, a visiting professor of infectious disease.

Another mark of her renown in pediatric infectious disease was being invited to edit the Red Book, a diagnostic manual. As a doctor friend told me, the Red Book is "the most authoritative reference manual" that practicing pediatricians use to diagnose infectious disease.

In Albany, Martha's work was varied. She ran the pediatric residency program and headed up the division of pediatric infectious disease. For a while, she chaired the pediatric department. Once again, she set up a virology lab. When HIV cases surfaced in the 1980s, she understood the research that was being conducted because the methodologies she had learned in Cleveland were still the gold standard.

"We were still learning about the virus and what it can do to a body. We knew almost nothing about how it affected infants. Some of the babies we saw in Albany were without families, essentially abandoned in the hospitals."

When Martha turned eighty, the local newspaper devoted an article to her. Here's a description one medical resident gave: "From a teaching perspective, she is the ideal attending physician. She will take the time to see patients with you and have a discussion with you after you see them." Young doctors were likely to take advantage of her kindness. "They know she won't be annoyed, even if they call her at eleven at night."[15]

In February 2020, at the start of the COVID-19 pandemic in the United States, I called Martha again. I wanted to know how she was doing and to hear what she thought about this new virus. As I expected, she was up on the news and was optimistic that scientists would develop a vaccine relatively quickly. She explained that the scientific basis for a vaccine today would be different from what it had been when she was a young doctor. The field of genetics had exploded, and a new vaccine would rely on genetic codes, rather than the virus itself, to produce antibodies.

At the same time, she knew that some people would be hesitant about a vaccine. Even before COVID-19, she had warned about adults who refused to have their children vaccinated. "Inoculation against the older diseases has been pivotal in eradicating them, or keeping them at bay, and we need to remain vigilant. There are now two generations of parents who never knew polio. Today's antagonism toward immunization is because they've never seen polio and the other diseases. They don't know what they can do to children."

It is hardly surprising that Martha has received numerous honors and awards over the course of her career. Honored

ILLUS. 4.4   Dr. Martha Lepow and Dr. David Clark holding newborn twins, 2000. Photograph courtesy of Albany Med Health System.

ILLUS. 4.5 Martha Lepow and her daughter, granddaughter, and great granddaughters, undated. Photograph courtesy of Martha Lepow.

by Western Reserve as a distinguished alumna, by Albany Medical College for excellence in teaching, and by the American Association of Pediatrics for lifetime achievement, she was also an endowed chair recipient at Albany Medical Center and active in many medical societies and civic organizations. Oberlin College awarded her an honorary degree in 2009, which particularly pleased her. "I got opportunity from Oberlin. If I hadn't gone there, I might not have been accepted at a medical school, but in college I was surrounded by people who loved learning, as I did, and were enthusiastic about what they were doing. When you get something like that, you want to see it perpetuated. Life is finite, but while I can, I want to keep things moving along, for children and grandchildren. Mine and all of ours."

When Martha went to Connecticut in the 1970s, the number of women attending medical school had surged. In one sense, this put her in good company. But there was a crucial difference: she was practically a generation older than the women who were just setting out to become doctors. She had started in medicine when women were not even close to being a critical mass. She knew from the outset that she would be part of a two-career couple: she and Lee assured her father of this when they married. It was up to them to figure out how to make it work. Despite having clear objectives for herself, Martha also knew when her career and her family needed her to change course, so that she ended up with both, intact and enhanced.

Intermezzo

Because I Was a Girl

In high school, I made, at best, spotty progress toward a career that would earn me respect and authority. The second wave of feminism was building, but I was only dimly aware of it. I was more interested in miniskirts and rock 'n' roll.

In my junior year, my math teacher suggested I take calculus. Like Martha Lepow, I thought girls were not supposed to be good in math. I said no, even though the very reason she encouraged me was that I had shown aptitude.

When I wanted to run for student council president, a boy in my class told me that was a job for a boy. He had himself in mind, of course. He was popular with the class and likely to win, but he was clearing the field of any viable challenger. Gullible and susceptible, I backed away.

When I was a senior, my guidance counselor suggested I apply to a two-year college. Even I, who had already swallowed other ideas about how a girl should limit herself, thought this was a bad idea. Not only did I have good grades but my parents were firm believers in higher education. My father was the first in his family to go to college, and his life was an object lesson in the avenues that opened because of education. But it was my mother who really put her foot down. She had gone to a junior college and would hear of nothing but four years for me. Even if my guidance counselor thought two years was enough for a girl, my mother did not.

In college, I majored in art history, partly because of my mother's influence. When I was young, she had taken me to many museums. At the Museum of Fine Arts in Boston, my favorite room was the one with dim light, a creaky floor, and Egyptian mummies. In eighth grade, when we studied ancient Egypt and could choose a topic for a paper, I wrote about Egyptian stone carvings. In other classes where we could pick a subject, I always chose art. My mother audited art history classes at Wellesley College and showed me illustrations in her textbook, H. W. Janson's *History of Art,* to explain what she was learning.

At Oberlin, the art history department was housed in a rectangular building with an interior courtyard. I liked to get a desk next to a window so I could look out into the courtyard; even in winter, bare branches were beautiful against the stucco gray walls. Studying art history means having command over lots of facts. Dates, locales, political history, mythological figures, and religious personages—they all matter. But there is also the feeling of transcendence that comes from looking at certain pieces of art. Sometimes I felt I had been transported to another culture and could understand what it was like to live in another time. Some nights I dreamed I existed in a landscape painting I had seen that day. Years later, when I saw the movie *The Mill and the Cross,* in which a Brueghel painting comes to life, it made perfect sense to me. I had seen paintings come to life in my dreams, and I had been in them.

I took a broad range of classes—European baroque, American modern, Asian and African art. In the summers, I interned at the Worcester Art Museum and Boston's Isabella Stewart Gardner Museum. When I finished college, I thought I would become a museum curator.

5

The Age of Sputnik

Mildred Spiewak Dresselhaus, Physicist

(b. 1930)

REDS FIRE 'MOON' INTO SKY. This was the October 5 headline in the *Chicago Daily Tribune* in the year 1957. The print was bold and extra large, designed to reflect the fear that engulfed the country. The Cold War had reached a new fever pitch, and the United States was losing.

The "moon" of the headline was the Soviet satellite Sputnik, the first man-made object to orbit the earth. It would be a while before the Eisenhower administration could assess the true dimensions of the threat, but as propaganda, the launch was an immediate success. It raised the specter of spies and attacks coming from space and knocked Americans off their self-satisfied perch. Sputnik was a demonstration of Soviet, not American, superiority in science and engineering.[1]

On that day, Mildred Spiewak was a student at the University of Chicago, a year away from getting her PhD in physics. Poised by virtue of her education to take advantage of the doors that would open because of Sputnik, she was a rare woman. Rarer still was the extraordinary success she later achieved when her work with carbon, then a little-appreciated material, helped fire up the field of nanotechnology and earn her a place as a full tenured professor at the Massachusetts Institute of Technology, the first woman with that distinction. Her nickname became "Queen of Carbon."

We met sixty years after the launch of Sputnik, but she remembered the punch it delivered. "It was a game changer," she told me. "And that had nothing to do with rockets. What it had to do with was the awakening of Americans that they were behind where they should be in science. Starting in 1960, the funding for science and math in school systems totally changed. It was realized that we had to produce more people in these fields to compete with the rest of the world or else we were going to fall behind."

To the kids in my neighborhood, Sputnik was a game. We heard it talked about on the news and listened to our parents debate its significance, but we were too young to take it seriously. When the sky darkened in the evenings, we were on the lookout: every light that moved or blinked in the sky could be Sputnik. We lay on the ground, our heads resting on a dog, a gentle black Lab from next door who liked nothing more than to have kids lounging on his belly. When we saw a light flicker, we would jump up, yell "Sputnik," and run after the tallest kid, who held a red ball high overhead. When we caught him, we would scramble for the ball, which was, in our imaginations, Sputnik. In truth, the satellite was only a little larger than our ball. We probably saw an airplane, a planet, or a twinkling star. But whatever it was, we were making ourselves part of the national conversation.

My meeting with Millie, as everyone called her, took place at MIT. The university buildings stretch along the Cambridge side of the Charles River, mostly monochromatic gray, labeled with numbers, seemingly cold and remote. Inside, one gets a different impression. The corridors were quiet as I walked to Millie's office, but I got glimpses that made me think differently about what went on here. Outside a professor's office, a few students huddled together on a bench, silently reading a tablet screen, intent and compatible. Farther on, a door opened, and three students hurried out of a florescent-lighted lab, bringing an air of intensity with them. They seemed engaged with each other and with whatever they had been doing in the lab. Down more corridors and around a corner, I spotted a sign for the "Dresselhaus Group." Articles about Millie and her husband, Gene Dresselhaus, also a physicist, covered the wall.

In her book *Lab Girl*,[2] Hope Jahrens describes the world of elite science as replete with doctorates and fellowships, endless grant applications, experiments that sound crazy but break new ground, and papers published for review by like-minded scientists. A professor with her own lab will supervise grad students, postdoc fellows, some undergraduates, and usually a technician or two. The group meets frequently, running experiments and socializing, in and out of the lab. Contrary to the notion that scientists make discoveries sequestered in a private lab, they tend to work closely with others, as much or more than anyone in business or law.

Jahrens, as an up-and-coming scientist, had to cadge lab equipment however she could, but Millie was far beyond that. By the time I met her, she had received a slew of honorary degrees and some of the most prestigious awards in science: the Kavli Prize in Nanoscience; the Enrico Fermi Award, an award from the American Chemical Society for encouraging women in science; the Oliver E. Buckley Condensed Matter Prize; the Oersted Medal; the Institute of Electrical and Electronics Engineers Medal; the National Medal of Science in Engineering; and the National Medal of Freedom. She was a former treasurer of the National Academy of Sciences, former president of both the American Physical Society and the American Association for the Advancement of Science, and a member of the National Academy of Engineering and the American Academy of Arts and Sciences. For a year she headed up the Office of Science within the U.S. Department of Energy.

Most of these honors recognized her work with carbon, the seemingly ordinary material in our pencils. When she discovered that graphene, a related material, can be cut into slices as thin as a single layer of atoms and be an excellent conductor of electricity, she helped propel nanotechnology—the creation of devices on an ultra-Lilliputian scale—into reality. For those of us who are not scientists, it is helpful to know that in nanotechnology, things are measured in nanometers, a unit equal to one-billionth of a meter. Picture the width of a human hair and conceive, if you can, that eighty thousand to one hundred thousand nanometer particles would have to be laid side by side to match the hair's width. Dealing with something so small is outside the normal experience of most people, but with electronics, that's what we rely on, whether we know it or not.[3]

When I walked into the Dresselhaus Group's suite of offices, I wanted to find out how Millie had succeeded so remarkably in science. Her assistant asked me to wait while she finished meeting with graduate students. Twenty minutes later, an inside door opened, two students walked out laughing, and I was shown into an office where books and papers covered all the tables and most of the chairs. Millie stood up from the desk, nodded at an empty seat, found another one for herself, and planted her feet on a small stool. Dressed simply in a long black skirt and sensible shoes, white hair braided and coiled on top of her head, she radiated energy.

When Millie was young, no one could have predicted that she would end up here. For one thing, very few women were awarded

ILLUS. 5.1 Mildred Dresselhaus in her MIT office, undated. Photograph courtesy of the Dresselhaus family.

doctorates—across all fields, only 10 percent went to women. In physics, she estimated, the figure was about 2 percent.[4]

Another thing was that she did not grow up with the advantageous home life other women in this book described to me. Her father did not show her the ropes of any profession, and her mother's jobs were menial. The family's goal was survival.

Her parents arrived in New York from Poland and Russia in the 1920s. They married a month later and started a family—Millie's brother and, in 1930, Millie. Her parents came from large families, but for themselves, they drew the line at two children. "People in Europe at that time had large families, but in ours there were just the two kids. I think my parents couldn't handle two very well, so it was a good idea to quit when they did. It was Depression time and it was tough going for them."

Tough going is an understatement. Millie's father was unwell for much of his life and always unemployed. "He spent some of his time in mental institutions, in and out," she said. "He didn't come to this country with any skills, and he didn't acquire any. He really never had a paying job to speak of."

Her mother became the family provider. "She was not raised with the expectation she would be the breadwinner, but as it turned out, she had no choice," Mille said. "When I was ten years old, my mother took a job in an orphanage. She would work a twelve-hour shift and then come home for twelve hours to see us briefly and sleep. After she worked in the orphanage, she got some factory jobs on an assembly line, working as an unskilled laborer."

At home, there were no toys, sometimes not enough food, and only one set of clothes for each child. Her mother washed the clothes at night and hung them up to dry, to have them ready for school the next morning. "We were on relief until I was about ten years old. That wasn't terribly uncommon during the Depression years. A lot of families were getting government support because there were no jobs. But still, it was a difficult existence."

Music was a spark in the family's life, a catalyst that helped Millie immeasurably. "In the ghettos in Europe, my father's family had been cantors," she said. "My father had an ear for music, and a good voice too, although he never became a cantor." But he sang and taught himself to play the violin. And, despite his difficulties, he recognized talent in Millie's older brother. "My brother was very gifted, in music and in everything—he taught himself how to read when he was just three years old. I followed in his footsteps, but I wasn't in his league. I was a precocious kid, but just normally precocious. He was really a prodigy.

"When my brother was three or four, my father took him to audition at the Bronx Music School. They had a famous teacher who was running a special program for children, and my brother won a scholarship for that. We were living in Brooklyn at the time, but we moved to the Bronx so my brother could go to this school. But six months after we moved, the teacher died, and the whole program collapsed. So there we were, dislocated, without any reason to be living in the Bronx. But since my parents had put all their resources into making the move, we had to stay. They didn't have the money to move again."

From what appeared to be a dead end, another possibility came into view—the music school at Greenwich House in Lower Manhattan. Founded in 1902, Greenwich House was one of the many settlement houses that thrived in cities, particularly where immigrants were numerous. The original concept was that better-educated and more affluent citizens would live in city houses, alongside the poor. They would learn what it was like to live in poverty, while offering educational and recreational services to those in need. Greenwich House, in the 1930s, ran on a somewhat different model. It had significant private patrons, including Eleanor Roosevelt, and money for scholarships.[5] Millie explained that when her father arranged for music lessons for his son, she also came into the school's orbit. "When my brother had lessons, the whole family would go with him, from the Bronx to Greenwich Village, by subway. And I would listen to his lesson, even though I was only two or three years old. One of the music teachers noticed me and thought I was gifted too, so I also got a scholarship."

If Millie had simply learned to play violin, her experience at Greenwich House would have been considered a success. But she got far more than that. Increasingly, as she got older, it gave her an entrée to a world far beyond her parents' ken. "For instance, when they wanted a kid who would be a movie critic, that was me. The other kids at music school didn't want to be bothered with tasks. But since I was a scholarship student, they could tell me what I was going to do, and they used to send me to movies and concerts to report on," and the reviews were published in the in-house newsletter. At one concert, she saw Leonard Bernstein conduct, very early in his career, when "he came in to pinch hit for somebody." She recalled writing in her review that this guy "was really amazing." She probably meant his 1943 debut with the New York Philharmonic. On the morning before the scheduled matinee, Bruno Walter realized he was too ill to conduct. Young Bernstein, then twenty-five, got the call to fill in. He visited the flu-stricken Walter, "wrapped up in blankets," to talk through the score. It was a challenging program that included Strauss's *Don Quixote*. As Bernstein remembered many years later, Walter noted "a few tricky spots where he cut off here but didn't cut off there; here you give it an extra upbeat, and so on."[6] At Carnegie Hall for the concert, Millie was part of the "warmly receptive" audience that was, by the finale, "wildly demonstrative."[7]

On a day when Eleanor Roosevelt visited Greenwich House, Millie was introduced. I imagine tea being served in the afternoon, ginger ale for the students, cookies on a tray. In her very distinctive voice, Mrs. Roosevelt would have asked the girl what she was studying. "Violin," Millie must have said, trying to sound confident, knowing that no one else from her neighborhood had ever met anyone so famous—not foreseeing that she herself would one day be a frequent visitor to the White House.

The music school staff were keen to see Millie get an education commensurate with her abilities. Aside from teachers at their children's school, her parents knew no one with a college degree. Strategies for getting their children a better education were unfathomable. But the teachers at Greenwich House did know the ropes, and they encouraged Millie to apply to Hunter College High School. The school had grown out of the teacher training school that Lydia Wadleigh once headed, after she left the 12th Street School where Mary Putnam studied science, as I learned from talking to Muriel Petioni.[8] Admission to the high school was based on test performance, and the music school staff gave Millie old exams for practice. For her, the test was easy, but she did not minimize the importance of having gotten in. "That was the big break of my whole life, I would say. That was the transformative step because it elevated me into a whole different level of society where I met other kinds of kids. It's supposed to be a cross section of New York, but it really isn't, because to get in, you need to have some background."

Architect Louis Kahn is said to have remarked that a great city is a place where a young person gets an idea of what he might like to do with his life.[9] Looking at Millie through this lens, we can see her as a young girl crisscrossing the city, traveling by subway to music class, Carnegie Hall, and the movies, and to meet Mrs. Roosevelt. None of this has anything to do with science, but it has everything to do with seeing that a wider world exists and is open to her. It is part of the background she needed to thrive in school and, later, in a career.

Her teachers in high school recommended Hunter College. "The curriculum was tailored for female careers. There was a strong bent towards the kind of jobs women might have a chance of doing—nursing, teaching, and secretarial. I assumed I was going to be a teacher."

But her interest in science put her on a different path. Unlike most of her classmates, she took classes with men. "Hunter College was a school for women only, but when I was there, they also took GIs returning from the war. That affected me much more than most people because I was doing science. The GIs were much more into science than they were in the other areas, so my classes were mixed."

Even more important was her physics teacher Rosalyn Yalow, who became a lifelong mentor. "The physics classes were tiny. Mostly, girls didn't take that subject, and when they got a student who was interested and able to do the problems, the teachers got interested. Rosalyn was interested in me."

The teacher may have seen something of herself in the student. Yalow's family, like Millie's, had Eastern European roots, and neither parent had finished high school. Her family could not afford to buy books, and every week she and her brother went to the public library to borrow a stack. Her parents wanted her to have a "practical career," preferably as an elementary school teacher, but she found science exciting. She remembered being a junior in college and "hanging from the rafters in Room 301 of Pupin Laboratories (a physics lecture room at Columbia

University) when Enrico Fermi gave a colloquium in January 1939 on the newly discovered nuclear fission." She recorded this memory in her biographical statement for the Nobel Prize, which she won in 1977 for her work developing the radioimmunoassay, a technique that measures antigens in the body.[10]

Even a scientist of Rosalyn Yalow's caliber had to finagle her way into graduate school. Her strategy was to strike a bargain: she would work as secretary to a biochemist, and he would help her get into graduate school. She mastered shorthand, he made good, and, in 1941, she entered the University of Illinois, happily tearing up her steno books. The first woman since 1917 to study at the engineering school, and the only woman among four hundred students, she understood that the coming war had created space for her. "The draft of young men into the armed forces, even prior to the American entry into the World War, had made possible my entrance into graduate school."

She gave Millie clear and direct advice: stick with science, and position yourself at the forefront of some field. It doesn't matter much which branch of science you are in, as long as you are in the forefront. She also told Millie to apply for a Fulbright grant after college, even though Millie had already been accepted at MIT for graduate work in math. The Fulbright came through, and Millie spent a year in England at the Cavendish Laboratory, which redirected her to science instead of math. Millie told me, "Any time Rosalyn suggested something, I just did it."[11]

After a year in Cambridge, England, Millie went to Cambridge, Massachusetts, for a master's degree in physics from Radcliffe College. Radcliffe was then a women's college, separate but affiliated with the all-male Harvard College, where most of the science classes were taught. At exam time, women students, no matter what they were studying, were corralled in a building on the Radcliffe campus. Millie remembered, "We were in a small room, and every single woman had a different examination. Harvard didn't want us around for the exams. We would have distracted the men, it was said."

Next, she went to the University of Chicago for a PhD. There she met Enrico Fermi, the Italian physicist who had emigrated in 1938, the year he won the Nobel Prize. In the United States, he continued his work with neutrons and eventually had a large role in developing nuclear energy and the atomic bomb. Twenty years after Rosalyn Yalow had been so excited to hear his lecture at Columbia, he taught quantum mechanics to her protégée. But it was outside the classroom that Millie managed to really get to know him. They lived near each other and, in the mornings, walked to school together. That half hour of exclusive quiet time with a great thinker was a tremendous opportunity. Fermi was versatile in physics and advised the same approach for Millie: get a broad exposure to the major subfields of physics and be equipped to do research in any area. "He taught me how to think about physics," she said. Also, having someone like Fermi in her corner could only help when she ran into opposition—someone like her advisor, for instance, who thought women did not belong in physics at all. According to him, women merely wasted resources better used for men.

The physics program was highly competitive for everyone. Millie explained how it worked. "They gave two exams. Fifty percent failed the first one, and the class was cut in half. Then the second year, we had another exam, and another fifty percent failed. In the end, only a quarter survived." Her memory echoed what my father said he heard in law school, long before the line was popularized in the movie *The Paper Chase*: look to your left, then look to your right; three years from now, only one of you will be here.

Millie not only survived the competitive atmosphere but did well. And she met Gene Dresselhaus, a theoretical physicist and junior faculty member. They were married, and when she graduated, they went to Cornell University, where Gene taught and Millie did a postdoc fellowship. They might have stayed, but Cornell made it clear that Millie would not be hired at the end of her fellowship. Gene decided it was more important for Millie to work than for him to stay, so they left Cornell.

When she began grad school, jobs in physics were hard to come by, and Millie thought she might go into research. But in her last year, things changed with Sputnik. MIT's Lincoln Laboratory, which was heavily engaged in defense research, had jobs for both her and Gene. "The guy who hired Gene and me wanted us individually to do what we did, for our different backgrounds. Gene was a theory person. I was an experimental person. We were hired not because we were a couple, but he was happy to get two people at once." On a staff of a thousand scientists, Millie was one of two women.

As seminal as Sputnik was, it was not the only thing to grab Americans' attention. In fall 1957, in the weeks before Sputnik, all eyes were on Little Rock, Arkansas, where nine Black students tried to enter Central High School, three years after the U.S. Supreme Court decision in *Brown v. Board of Education*. When screaming white mobs surrounded the students, President Eisenhower sent in the 101st Airborne Division to ensure that desegregation would proceed.

Then, on the very day that Sputnik went up, *Leave It to Beaver* premiered on American television. The show's vision of America was devoid of any Black character and empty of the fears Sputnik sparked. The Cleavers' family life was placid, except for the humorous escapades of the two boys, and it resonated with millions.

It is hard to imagine, though, that Millie paid any attention to June Cleaver. She was too busy with work and family. "I started working on carbon very soon after I got to Lincoln. It was kind of fluky. At first, I did what I was told. Everybody was doing semiconductors, so I did that too. And then, after five months of training and learning all the techniques, I said, gee, this is just like what everybody else is doing. Can't I do something more interesting than this?"

Gene gave her the idea to study carbon. "As part of his PhD thesis, he had done cyclotron resonance on graphite and carbon-related material and gotten some very good results and published a paper on it. Maybe you should try this, he suggested. I tried it, and it worked pretty well. Plus, it was different from what all these other guys were doing."

Working with carbon created an avenue to the broader field of condensed matter physics, then just emerging. "Condensed matter physics was nothing at that time. Almost nothing was known, and the field was just starting to break open, but the government figured that since the Russians were really strong in this field, we had better put a little bit of effort into it too. So my boss let me go into it. As long as I did some things that they wanted when they wanted, I could do my thing too. As I told you,

ILLUS. 5.2   Mildred Dresselhaus and her four children, undated.
Photograph courtesy of the Dresselhaus family.

we had Sputnik, and Lincoln Labs was very open to new ideas
because we had to get ahead of the Russians."

Things were busy at home too. Within six years, Millie and
Gene had four children, which meant they had to scramble to
keep things together. They hired a neighbor, Dorothy Terzian,
to take care of the kids. "She was sort of like my mother in the
sense that she did not expect, when she grew up, that she would
be a worker. They had five children in the family and couldn't
support them unless she worked. She had no training, so all
she could do was babysitting. Her youngest was five when she
started." She worked for Millie's family for twenty-nine years.

Even with regular, reliable childcare, the balancing act was
hard. "Everybody at the lab had to show up for work at eight
o'clock. No lateness allowed. By that time, we had four children.
We struggled for a year or two, and they kept complaining about
me. Gene and I came in at the same time, but nobody complained
too much about him. They were just complaining about me. I
was about to be fired."

Before she was fired, a fortuitous connection came into play.

From time to time, Millie had gone to MIT's main campus to use the magnet lab. There she met Arthur von Hippel, a professor in the electrical engineering department. He was from Germany and a music afficionado. "He decided that he was going to have a musical quartet for his lab," Millie said. "He was looking for a viola player and invited me to join the quartet. I'm not really a violist, but I play a bit." Joining the quartet was, like so many things in her life, an opportunity that brought unexpected rewards. "Von Hippel got to know my science. He suggested me as a faculty member. I would be on campus, and I could more easily play in his quartet."

Initially, her position was funded by the Abby Rockefeller Mauzé visiting professorship. In 1968, Millie was made a member of the electrical engineering faculty. Fifteen years later, she joined the physics faculty also and, in 1985, became the first woman to hold the title of Institute Professor, a mark of unusual esteem within the MIT community.[12]

Gene also left Lincoln Labs and moved to the main MIT campus. At home, he was uncommonly involved with the children. With Gene in the lead, cooking projects turned into chemistry lessons. Family photographs were an excuse to set up a dark room and talk about optics. The kids ran experiments with their chemistry set all the time, one after another. He and Millie took the kids to campus on the weekends, and their students came to the house.

One anecdote from the 1970s describes a day when Millie was working at home. Marianne, the oldest and then a teenager, was in charge when the phone rang. This is the story she told at a memorial event after her mother's death:

> "We're calling from the White House," the caller explained. "May we please speak to Professor Dresselhaus?"
>
> "No, you can't," I said, simply. "She's busy right now."
>
> The caller seemed a little confused. "This is the *White House*," the caller reminded me (in case I hadn't picked up on that). "Can you please tell Professor Dresselhaus that the White House is calling?"
>
> I was thoroughly unimpressed.
>
> "No," I said. "I'm sorry, but she's busy, and she gave me

strict instructions not to bother her. If this is for work, you can call her at the office on Monday."

"You have to understand, this is the *White House*," the caller explained again. "In Washington, D.C. If Professor Dresselhaus is there, we would really like to speak with her. Would you please put us through?"

"She *is* here," I replied, "but I can't put you through because I'm her daughter, and she gave me strict instructions that she's not to be disturbed right now, and that you should call back on Monday morning at her office."

It went on like this for a few minutes, the White House constantly insisting to me that they really were the White House and really did want to speak to Millie, while I stubbornly refused to let my mother be bothered.

Finally, they conceded. "We'll call back on Monday."

When my mother came downstairs, she asked if anything important had happened while she was busy.

"Nothing really important," I answered, with a shrug. "You got a phone call, but I told them you were busy and couldn't be disturbed, and they said they'd call back on Monday."

On Monday morning, the White House did call her office and managed to speak with her. The first thing they said, when they got through, was how much they had enjoyed talking to her daughter on the phone, because when people from the White House call professors, they're always put through immediately. They'd never had a child tell them "No, I'm sorry, but my mother is very busy right now. She can't be interrupted!" It tickled them pink.

When my parents got home and told me this, I frowned and asked them if I'd done the right thing.

"It was the Nixon White House," my dad told me. "So yes. You did. Hang up on them more often, Marianne."[13]

At work, Millie had few women colleagues, and none in the electrical engineering department when she joined. "It wasn't just that there weren't many women. It was a zero set at that time," she said. Only 4 percent of MIT's students were women. Dispersed across the university in various departments, they

ILLUS. 5.3   Mildred and Gene Dresselhaus in La Napoule, France, at the first international conference on intercalation, 1977. Photograph courtesy of the Dresselhaus family.

had little sense of community with other women. Emily Wick, the first woman to earn tenure at MIT, was also associate dean of students, and she decided to do something about it. "Emily Wick was very influential," Millie said. "She wanted to build up a support structure for the few women we had. So we started a program." The Women's Forum, which began in 1972, convened faculty, staff, and students to talk about issues of particular relevance to women, from health to career options. Millie ran a popular seminar on roles for women in science and engineering and, in 1973, received a Carnegie Foundation grant to encourage women in science.

Given her own success as a scientist, Millie had a unique role to play when it came to other women. She generously mentored her students and advocated widely for women across the spectrum of science. Yet, from what I have learned about her, she was a scientist first. In other words, she championed other women because she believed that enlarging the pool of talent and rolling out the welcome mat would help science.

She was very proud of what science had done for society. When we talked about the many jobs created in the wake of Sputnik, she praised that generation of scientists whose work created opportunities for people today. "That's why you have so much prosperity," she said. "I don't know that law makes prosperity. Somebody has to pay the lawyers with something." Her comment took me by surprise. We hadn't been discussing the relative merits of science and law, or talking about law at all. I said I thought law had intrinsic value in society but did not push it further.

Millie also looked to science for explanations. Her grand-daughter Leora, a grad student at MIT, shared this memory of Millie. "As young girls," Leora said, "my sister and I went on science adventures together with our mother or grandmother. We were always encouraged to be curious about our surround-ings and to try to learn how things worked. . . . In family and in mentoring, Millie always led by example. I'm certain that she inspired the family spirit that science holds answers to the world around us. It wasn't until later in my life that I started to understand that other young girls got very different childhood messages."[14]

It is not hard to see how Millie, together with Gene, inspired the family to think about science. What is less obvious is how Millie herself caught the bug for science. Her earliest influences—family, Bronx public schools, music classes—were unrelated. Maybe she was hard-wired for science. It is also the case that she was an uncommonly bright girl who caught the attention of teachers who were in a position to help. She wisely

ILLUS. 5.4 Mildred Dresselhaus at the White House to receive the National Medal of Freedom, 2014. Photograph courtesy of Barack Obama Presidential Library.

accepted their help, beginning with the music teachers who guided her toward an excellent high school and gave her things to be curious about, such as movies and concerts. This, she mused, might explain some of her success.

Reflecting on the fact that she cut a higher profile than Gene, she had this to say: "When we started out, he was well ahead of me, but as time went on, it just happened that things I was working on worked out better or whatever. I don't know what it is. My music. I don't know. I'm telling you that whatever you know sort of comes in. My music came in at some very key places in my career. And not only with von Hippel. I had all the experience doing all this stuff for the music school. That turned out to really broaden my experiences and teach me about innovation and doing things, figuring out things to do that are not advertised. You know, new directions that you sort of engineer yourself."

Toward the end of our meeting, Millie asked about my approach. "So you focus a lot on the early years, on how people get into what they're doing?" She was right. I do believe that what happens in our early years is paramount. Something obvious, such as who your parents are, shapes us. More subtle things—an attitude you pick up, a feeling that grabs you, an event that seems inconsequential at the time but resurfaces years later—can also have an effect. Out of the myriad things that occur in the hundred thousand hours we spend as children, we cannot know what will stick or make a difference. Because so many possibilities lie hidden there, childhood is the haystack where I always search for needles to explain the spark of ambition.

For Millie, her innate intelligence, her devoted mentors, and the fortuitous timing of events were instrumental. But I also think her parents played a role in her success. They were not in a position to coach her on scientific experiments, or even to guide her quest for higher education, but they made unique contributions. Her father, unable to support his family financially, was discerning about music. When he spotted talent in his older child, he found a music school to cultivate it. That triggered a series of events that changed the trajectory of Millie's life. Her connection to the social safety net, in this case, Greenwich House and its teachers, was a significant step toward acquiring "background," as she put it, and that, in turn, put her in position to acquire a rigorous education. Without her father fortuitously starting her down that path of connections, her life undoubtedly would have been different.

Her mother was also key. She adapted to a life she never envisioned for herself, working long hours at menial jobs to keep the family going. Under the strain and fatigue that must always have been with her, she maintained a fundamental sense of optimism, which Millie mused about in our conversation. "You know, I was very lucky. I had one parent who made things work and had kind of a vision—that the kids somehow would do better than the parents. Not knowing what or how but that, somehow, it was going to happen." Millie seemed to have picked up her mother's optimism and her refusal to feel defeated, even in adversity. That outlook may have led Millie to achievements that exceeded, by multiples, her mother's faith that things would get better.

Intermezzo

Turning Point

My first job after college was at Advent Corporation. Part established business, part start-up, the company manufactured stereo speakers and was developing a projection television set. I was hired for an entry-level job as administrative assistant to two vice presidents, where I answered phones, typed letters, booked appointments, and generally tried to keep the two men organized. Organization was nearly impossible. My bosses were considered brilliant at marketing, but they were also a mess, even if you consider the place (Cambridge), the time (the mid-1970s), and the context (a scrappy audio engineering company founded by the legendary Henry Kloss, best known as the K of KLH).

For writing phone messages, I had a book with alternating white and yellow pages, the yellow embedded with carbon that retained a copy of my handwritten message. After a call came in, I would lay the message on top of the desk of whichever of my bosses it was for, where piles of papers looked as though they had exploded. I would wait a discreet interval before asking if he had returned the call. Usually he had not, and the frustrated caller would be on the line again, later that day and the next. Caught in the middle and unable to handle the caller's concern myself, I was far away from an ideal job.

Before taking this one, I was offered a job at the Museum of Fine Arts. That also would have been entry level and administrative, meaning I would type, which was true of most jobs for young women in those days. Maybe it would have led somewhere else, but probably not to a curatorship, because, as I had belatedly figured out, I would need a PhD for that. Not ready to commit myself to a doctoral program, I decided to try the business world, and that's how I found my way to Advent. The job was not glamorous, but I'd hoped it might lead to something better.

It did not. Truthfully, my knowledge and skills were not a good match for the company. I knew little about audio and nothing about electrical engineering, and I was unequipped for anything requiring technical expertise. On the business side, I had not studied finance or accounting and had little aptitude for sales.

Another stumbling block was that everyone at the top was a man. A few of the company's women had titles that suggested a senior status, but in reality, they played supporting roles. I carefully observed the two most senior women at work and saw that they exercised little authority of their own. Even if I did acquire skills or knowledge that would be useful to the company, I would not have the kind of role I wanted.

There was one other thing, which I mention as an aside. About a year into the job, one of my bosses said it was time for my annual performance evaluation. He asked me to meet him after work so we could talk about it. That seemed a little strange, but not so strange that I said no. He suggested we meet at a bar. Also strange, but I did not say no to that either. But when I felt his hand on my thigh, I did say no. There was no way I was going to let him be intimate with me. Of all the negative thoughts that followed, and there were many, it never occurred to me that saying no might affect my job. If it had, I still would have said no. I stayed for almost another year.

Not because of that, but because I wanted a more interesting job, I began to think about options. Go to a new city and make a new start, maybe. I spent months deliberating a move to New York or Philadelphia before realizing what should have been obvious—changing cities is not the same as building a career. Since I was already in the business world, I thought about getting an MBA. An acquaintance had recently graduated from Harvard Business School, and when he talked about his job marketing Gillette shavers, I tried to picture myself in a job like his. He was enthusiastic, but I was unable to identify a core in his work that was inherently interesting to me.

Law, of course, was an option, but I had been so intent on finding my own way that I had not considered it. As much as I loved and admired my father, I did not want to copy him. But I was steeped in his approach. Around the family dinner table we talked about the issues of the day, including civil rights, the war in Vietnam, Watergate. Our discussions often touched on legal concepts—how law functioned, its role in government, and why it mattered to society. As Mildred Dresselhaus and her family looked to science for explanations, my family looked to the rule of law.

Neither of my siblings went into law, but they were as affected by the family ethos as I was. Though my brother works in finance, he avidly follows government policy and politics, including the attendant legal questions. Our sister died when she was a senior at Georgetown University, but I am sure she would have had a career in the State Department or elective office.

Still working at Advent and bumbling along in my quest for a career, a question from a friend brought clarity. We were talking about our future job prospects when he asked what I wanted to accomplish by the time I was thirty. I was in my mid-twenties, and all of a sudden, his question revealed that it was time to get on with things. And law, I came to see, was a good option: it suited my interests and abilities, it did not require that calculus class I never took, and it would give me expertise that was a foundation for building a career. I took a new job as a paralegal and, in my one year at a law firm, took the LSAT, investigated different law schools, prepared my applications, and applied for a loan.

I began law school at Boston University in 1977. It was the height of second wave feminism, when the number of women in graduate school and professional jobs rose sharply. My father's copy of *Black's Law Dictionary* was still on my parents' bookshelf, and I took it to my apartment. His was the third edition, copyright 1933, already superseded by newer editions. But really, how much updating did these archaic legal words need? Even if some definitions had been updated, I was determined to use his book. I still have it.

My father and I started having conversations about torts and property law, standard first-year subjects. He told me anecdotes about his experiences in law school, and I told him what I was doing. In my third year, I took a class on banking law, where there is a dense universe of statutes and regulations, very dry. But for me, it was also about understanding, finally, what my father did at the office. I must be the only person on the planet who has ever found that the study of banking law made her feel closer to another human being.

Time for Change

Frieda Garcia, Nonprofit Leader

(b. 1932)

Several times a week, I walk from South End to the Back Bay to do errands, visit the library, or meet a friend. On my route, I pass the Frieda Garcia Park, a small city park tucked next to a side street. Playground equipment, benches, and shade trees make it an oasis for kids and adults. Bright murals line one side of the park, yellow, orange, green, and blue, as vibrant as the woman for whom the park is named.[1]

What sort of accomplishment earns the honor of having a park bear your name? For Frieda Garcia, it was her uncommon dedication to making city life better—leader of social service organizations; member of nonprofit boards, from the richly endowed to the struggling; a deft touch with politicians and corporate power brokers; fluent in cultural competence, before the term was even coined. She swept aside the unspoken boundaries of a hide-bound and racially divided city. Yet, despite her accomplishments, Frieda was modest when I asked her for an interview.

"I don't quite fit in the box," she said, meaning she was not a doctor, lawyer, or scientist, the examples I had given in the introductory email explaining my project. She was also hesitant because her path had not been straight. "I was born in the Dominican Republic. This cultural thing is going to interfere a little bit with my story," she added. Without knowing exactly what she meant by "this cultural thing," I assured her that her swerves and false starts would be as interesting as someone else's beeline to a career.

Our first conversation took place in my living room. I brought out glasses of water, sliced fruit, and cookies, but our conversation became so animated that we touched nothing. I came to realize that animated was Frieda's default setting.

In 1941, when she was eight years old, Frieda left Santo Domingo, the city where she was born, and arrived in New York City with her mother and brother. Ostensibly, they came for medical consultations. "My brother had problems—epilepsy and some mental incapacity," Frieda told me. "That was sort of the reason we came, to see some doctors." But the trip became a springboard to a new life in the United States, where her mother could be free of an unhappy marriage. Social taboos would have defined her life had she been a separated or divorced woman in the Dominican Republic. "If my mother had stayed, she would have had to live with her parents. I don't think she ever planned to go back." New York offered an enticing freedom.

In her passport photo, Frieda wears a dress her mother made—intricately styled, belted, and embroidered and finished with a bolero-length braided jacket. "My mother barely knew how to cook, but the one thing she had been taught was sewing." As with Muriel Petioni's mother, that skill would allow her to earn an income in her new country.

No one in the family spoke English when they arrived. Her grandparents had arranged for them to live with a Dominican acquaintance in the Bronx. "But when my mother got there," Frieda remembered, "she assessed the situation and decided it was not a good one. The person was receiving welfare and getting some rent money from us, and whenever the welfare person came around, we were supposed to hide. We moved within a few months."

ILLUS. 6.1 Frieda Garcia, her mother, and her brother in their passport photo, circa 1941. Photograph courtesy of Frieda Garcia.

They went to Upper Manhattan, Frieda's base for years to come. Everyone around them spoke Spanish, but the slang and accents varied block by block. "What I remember is 108th Street was sort of Cuban, 109th was mostly Puerto Rican, and 110th, where we lived, was Dominican. My mother never did learn to speak English, but within about two months, I was thoroughly bilingual. That's the way it happens when you're eight."

As the English-speaking child, she grew up quickly, interpreting at family medical appointments and filling out official forms. Her language proficiency meant that she could travel around the city independently. "With my brother, whom I adored and who had a kind of photographic memory, we wandered all over the place. We never got lost and went everywhere," she said. Of all the places they went, she liked the library best. "I could walk to the public library, about nine blocks away. I read all the time. That really saved me." Books fed her intellectual curiosity, and that she would have to safeguard in the face of others' assumptions about what a girl should do with her life.

She also acquired status in the neighborhood. Other families asked for help navigating their paperwork, and when she was older, she babysat for their children. Being in charge came naturally to Frieda. When the young children complained that she made them eat vegetables, she just laughed.

Her mother got a factory job making military supplies during the war. Frieda also remembered her crafting hand-sewn lamp shades. Together, they went to a hotel room, where her mother fitted a gown on a client before bringing it home to stitch the hand-rolled hem. Sometimes her mother received a money transfer from the family back home.

The local public school that Frieda attended served an immigrant population. "The kids came from all over. This was the 1940s, and people were coming from Europe to get away from Hitler. They spoke all different languages," she said. "We were all together in one class and since we couldn't speak the others' languages, we learned English. The only person who spoke English as a native was the teacher."

Of course, learning to speak the language is not the same as learning to speak up for yourself. "The problem, when you're in a public school and your mother doesn't speak English," she said, "is that nobody is running interference for you. When I was in the sixth grade, I realized that some of my friends were in what appeared to be a more advanced class." Reflecting back, she realized that in her desperation to grow up, she conveyed a certain impression of herself to her teachers. "I wore my mother's earrings to school, and the teachers would pull them off. I don't know if *demoted* is the word, but the teachers thought I wasn't interested in education. They put me in the commercial class so I could be a secretary."

But not for long did she worry about teachers who underestimated the brown-skinned girl who wore a woman's earrings. "Around this time, I met a friend of the family who was in a convent boarding school. I decided that was what I wanted to do. My mother was not enthused, but it was something I wanted to do, and I guess I was pretty strong-headed." With the sporadic payments that came from home, plus her earnings, Frieda's mother had enough to send her to boarding school at Mount Saint Dominic Academy in Caldwell, New Jersey.

Away from home, Frieda was miserable. "I was twelve, in seventh grade, and crying all the time. I got my period two months into the school year and had to deal with the nuns and all that nonsense." When the first semester ended, the nuns asked her mother to come for a conference. "With my mother sitting there, the principal turned to me and asked if I wanted to stay. 'We can't have you crying all the time,' she said. And that did it. I said I wanted to stay."

She realized that she liked learning about American culture. "I had been living in the United States but not living a truly American life. At home, it was strictly Dominican. Food. The whole family structure. The friends. Everything Dominican. I remember vividly the first time I had applesauce, something we never had at home. My god. I loved it." In June, when the school year ended, Frieda cried again, this time because she had to go home.

As Frieda was enjoying American tastes and culture, her mother was worrying she would stray too far. "My mother had two goals for me," Frieda said. "One was that I be married off as a virgin. Otherwise, I would be returned. The second was that I not marry an American because an American man would put her in a nursing home when she got old. Spanish men didn't do that. Those were her only goals."

Also, the ideal son-in-law would not want a well-educated, independent wife. "My mother would tell me at night to turn off the light—you're going to go blind. Nobody is going to want to marry you. She was worried I would be too intellectual, too well read."

Frieda let some of her mother's advice roll off her back. She was, after all, the girl who insisted on picking her own school. But other advice lodged deep inside, eventually to influence some of the decisions that lay ahead.

For a while, Frieda considered becoming a nun. The Dominican sisters who ran the school seemed to have a calm, contemplative life centered on education. Her mother put a stop to that. She told Frieda, "Our family is not very good at celibacy."

At a school conference, the nuns asked her mother what she thought Frieda should do after high school. "In the family," Frieda said, "everybody's idea was that I should become a secretary. That was the ultimate. But the nuns said no, 'Frieda is college material.'"

"I was already on the college track, learning Latin and everything I needed. When I was accepted at Fordham University, all the neighbors were shocked, because in those days, Spanish kids weren't accepted to college." But once she was there, she did not find the intellectual stimulation she had hoped for. "What I remember about Fordham was memorizing and being able to recite the complete works of Thomas Aquinas in Latin. Other things were taught, but that is what I remember."

Partway through college, she met a Dominican man named John who was living in downtown Manhattan. "His father had a ranch back home," Frieda said. "He sent John up to the States to mature and straighten out. A lot of families did that with their sons. John wanted to get married, and my mother was thrilled. I was lukewarm. I wasn't really in love, as I realized when I met with a priest a couple of days before the marriage. But I went through with it."

She soon dropped out of college. "We lived at home with my mother. And it was just—it was a mess. And of course, there was the virginity part. I kept the blood-stained wedding gown for years."

It was, and is, de rigueur in many cultures for a woman to be a virgin when she marries. This imperative had been drilled into Frieda for years. And virginity was not a purely private status. It had to be proven with evidence, such as the red-stained dress, the only way she could avoid being "returned" as damaged goods.[2]

Along with social customs, Dominican politics came into play. Frieda asked if I knew about Rafael Trujillo, who ruled the Dominican Republic as a brutal dictator for thirty years. She explained that he made a practice of installing experienced people as the heads of commercial enterprises. When an enterprise turned successful, Trujillo would oust his hand-picked director and take all the credit. Even though everyone knew how things would play out, all agreed to go along with the plan because, really, there was no choice with someone like him. "When Trujillo wanted to get into the cattle business, he hired John's father to buy a cattle farm. The plan was to train John to be part of that, so his father sent us down to Ocala, Florida, where John worked at a ranch. Eventually, we went to the Dominican Republic, where we were installed on a ranch in the middle of nowhere, without running water or electricity. Once a month, I went into town to buy food, but otherwise, I was out in the countryside with only the workers."

Frieda was not expected to do ranch work per se, but she was much too energetic to do nothing. She started a school for children of the ranch workers and, at night, taught the workers themselves. "It was like the Peace Corps," she said.

In this isolated environment, the marriage started to fray. "I was still super Catholic at this time. With a priest who lived nearby, we built a sort of frame of a church, and he came every Sunday to say Mass. I became a third order Carmelite, which means that I wore a scapular, not regular dresses, and said certain prayers every day. I sent away to Spain for a Lady of Mt. Carmel statue. John, in the meantime, decided to take up with somebody in town. He came to *me* to consult as to whether or not she was a virgin. *Insane.*"

Finally, Frieda had had enough. When her mother and grandfather came to visit, she decided to leave the ranch altogether. "We got a Jeep, which we needed because it had been raining for weeks and everything was flooded. I left with my bloody wedding dress and the statue of the Virgin, which my mother carried." On their way out the door, her mother took the opportunity to confront John: "Everything Frieda predicted you would do, you have done."

It must have been difficult for Frieda's mother to see her daughter in this position. Marriage, with all the traditional trappings, had not turned out any better for Frieda than it had for her. Yet generations-old values are not easily overthrown; they linger, to define our perceptions and guide our actions. It is therefore not surprising that Frieda's family viewed her prospects through a very traditional lens. "When I got back to New York," she said, "I was twenty-six years old, separated, and then divorced. My life was over, by Dominican standards."

Her American life was in jeopardy too. Although she had been a citizen since she was a child, her American citizenship was revoked after she voted in a Dominican election, even though that was legal. "This was one of the lowest points in my life," she said. "Even though I was a citizen, and this is the country where I had spent most of my life, voting got me classified as a visitor, which meant I couldn't work. I had to go to my congressman to get that straightened out."

From there, she took a step forward. "Finally, I went to secretarial school. I hadn't finished college, but I needed a job. Then I got a job at Ideal Publishing that put out a third-rate movie magazine." Finally, she had a job her family thought was right for her.

Teen Time's audience was teenaged girls.[3] It carried fan club news and reported on events like the Junior Miss pageant and Chubby Checker's appearance at the Copacabana, where he danced the twist. Midtown Manhattan, as Frieda described it, was like the set of the television show *Mad Men*. "A lot of things on the show were very familiar," she told me. "The drinking, for one thing. Everybody came back from lunch a little tipsy because they had martinis. Up and down Madison Avenue were bars. They were packed at lunch and again at the end of the day." Frieda herself wasn't much of a drinker. "I never went in except the day JFK was sworn in. I decided to treat myself to lunch at a bar so I could watch the inauguration on television."

Another thing that rang true in the show was the predominance of men. "The whole publishing industry and the PR firms were all men. My boss, Julia Ransom, had her job because it was about fashion and celebrities. That made it sort of a woman's job. But mostly it was men."

One other similarity was evident. As some cultural critics have noted, the show's female characters evolved: while the male characters remained stuck in ruts both personal and professional, women like Joan Holloway and Peggy Olson showed surprising talents and the ability to grow into positions of power. They were fictional characters, but Frieda's real life ran parallel—she took stock of the situation and decided how to grow beyond expectations.[4]

"My goal was to get my bachelor's degree so I could be a social

ILLUS. 6.2   Cover of *Teen Time*, August 1962. Copyright Romance Pub. Corp.

worker," she said. "That would be a continuation of what I had done all along, as the English-speaking child who went to medical appointments and offices." Fordham, however, was not the right place for her. Instead, she enrolled at the New School for Social Research, a much better fit. She could take classes at night and have the kind of stimulating discussions she had always wanted. Many of the faculty members were refugees from fascism and the war in Europe, and they made class exciting. "On Friday nights I had a Russian teacher teaching me Russian literature. The class wouldn't end 'til 9:30, but I would have stayed 'til midnight. I loved reading—books like *War and Peace*. Everything. Everything." Most of the professors and students shared a progressive political outlook.

Earl Warren, chief justice of the U.S. Supreme Court, was the speaker at Frieda's 1964 graduation. The Court had already issued landmark decisions in the areas of desegregation, criminal justice, and school prayer, and protestors met him on arrival. "Earl Warren hates white people—we won't mix," they chanted. "We want to pray in school, Earl Warren," and "Earl Warren is a sneaky red."

Inside, the chief justice thanked the graduates for their hospitality. "I even appreciate the hospitality of that reception committee on the outside," he said. "Thank goodness we live in a free country where people can say what they want, even when it is ill mannered at times." He spoke about the open exchange of ideas as an underlying value of our society. Nowhere, he said, given our diversity, does the motto *E Pluribus Unum* have greater national significance than in the United States.[5]

Back at *Teen Time*, Frieda's boss, who had become a friend, introduced her to her nephew. Timothy Wright, an intellectual and an aesthete whose grandfather was the architect Frank Lloyd Wright, was dramatically unlike Frieda's first husband. That may have been part of the attraction. Frieda and he were married in Bethesda, Maryland, in a house designed by his grandfather.

Timothy worked at the publishing company G. P. Putman. One night, he and Frieda attended a reception for star author John le Carré. "I was the only person of color," Frieda said. "I have never felt so ostracized in my whole life." It did not help that other women at the party openly flirted with her husband.

Awareness of distinctions based on color and ethnicity was nothing new for Frieda. In Florida with her first husband, she had seen segregation, legal and enforced. "We lived in a rooming house that no Black would ever have been allowed to live in. At the movies, the balcony was always said to be under construction, and that's where Black people had to sit." But in Florida, she and her husband were exempt from those restrictions. "Although I consider myself to have Black characteristics, John did not look Black. Also, because we spoke Spanish and had some means, we could go anywhere." At a New York publishing party, the line of demarcation was more nuanced, but she knew the line existed. Bridging it would be part of her life's work.

Frieda and Timothy moved to Chicago for his graduate program in history. She took the state licensing exam for social workers, got a job in clinical microbiology while she waited for the results, and, once she passed, worked in the Cook County welfare office. "For someone who grew up in New York, I was learning about America. And I was living it. A coworker had a boat, and we spent weekends on the river. It was a wonderful experience." When Timothy was accepted into a doctoral program at Harvard, they moved again.

"I knew three things about Boston when I moved," she said, "Paul Revere, Edward Brooke, who was then the state's Black senator, and Isabella Stewart Gardner and her museum. My boss at the magazine wore big hats and looked like her." Such images suggested the city would be more progressive than it was. In 1965, she found it to be a "pretty mean place."

The city was mean in a physical sense. The Prudential Building, then the tallest building anywhere outside of New York City, had just opened, but much of the urban infrastructure was neglected. In the name of urban renewal, several neighborhoods had been knocked down, leaving some tracts vacant; others had become industrial sites or windswept, uninhabited plazas. Displaced residents struggled to regain a sense of community.

It could also be mean in a human sense, and that's really what Frieda meant. For decades, city politicians and corporate leaders, at least some of them, had wielded power to preserve prerogatives for themselves and other kindred, white groups. An exodus of jobs left city residents underemployed. Residential redlining left many Boston neighborhoods racially and ethnically homogeneous, not heterogeneous.

Growing up in a suburban town, I formed my own impression of Boston. My family visited the city, and I had summer jobs there. My sense was that the energy, money, and jobs that were once concentrated in Boston were dispersed, including among the technology companies that ringed Route 128. The urban neighborhoods that endured were often balkanized enclaves built on ethnic identity. Two books buttressed my impression. *Death at an Early Age,* published in 1967, is Jonathan Kozol's account of teaching fourth grade in a public school in Roxbury. His class met in the corner of an auditorium, not in a dedicated classroom. If there were books, they were old and soiled. Misbehaving children were swatted on the hand with rattan. When some students came to school obviously hungry or with signs of abuse, school officials averted their eyes. I read Kozol's book when I was in high school, with my parents' encouragement, and it introduced me to de jure and de facto segregation, terms that were new to me but highly relevant to any discussion of race.

Then there was the seminal *Common Ground* by J. Anthony Lukas. He covered the fallout from the 1972 federal lawsuit *Morgan v. Hennigan,* which sought to desegregate Boston public schools. The action took place in the decade after Frieda arrived in Boston, but the racially divided city Lukas described is what she first encountered. The focal point was the court order, issued in 1974, that students be bused to schools outside their neighborhoods to achieve racial balance. The order sparked protests and violence, which affected students, teachers, politicians, and, really, the whole city. Lukas recounted the experience of three families in very different neighborhoods: South Boston, which was mostly white; Roxbury, which was mostly Black; and the South End, a mixed neighborhood on the verge of gentrification. The busing crisis, as it is often called, made Boston notorious.

At the same time, Boston and adjacent Cambridge had a vibrant counterculture. Hippies lived in communes and on the streets. Crowds marched on Boston Common to protest the war in Vietnam. A woman's collective published *Our Bodies, Ourselves,* a book that advocated self-knowledge about women's bodies. Joan Baez and Taj Mahal sang at Club 47. The Jazz Workshop and Paul's Mall hosted Miles Davis, BB King, and other jazzers. Van Morrison, Johnny Winter, and the Velvet Underground played rock venues like the Boston Tea Party.

But in 1965, when Frieda was first in Boston, she could not find a job. Her dream was to work at the Roxbury Multi-Service Center, a new organization that offered comprehensive services to the mostly Black population of Roxbury, but they required social workers to have a master's degree. Lacking that, she looked to Boston's welfare department for a job. She wrote to the agency director, touting the fact that she was bilingual and had experience. She got silence. Follow-up phone calls brought only more silence. Months later, when she finally managed to land an interview, "the woman spent the entire interview trying to figure out how I could be married to someone who was going to Harvard." Once on the job, she witnessed her supervisor, nearly daily, berate clients who came for help. This was not how Frieda wanted to be of service.

A turning point came when she met Hubert Jones, known throughout the city as Hubie. Originally from the Bronx, he had come to Boston to study social work at Boston University. As assistant director of the Roxbury Multi-Service Center, soon to be director, he wanted to know more about Boston's growing Latino community. "Hubie had grown up in New York and had seen tensions between Latinos and Blacks," Frieda said. "He didn't want it repeated in Boston." He arranged for Frieda to be hired, even without a master's degree, as fact finder and liaison. Like Hubie, she was committed to building alliances between Black and Latino communities.[6]

One of the local initiatives Frieda discovered was La Alianza Hispana, a small organization started by two teachers in the late 1960s. It offered language and literacy programs to Spanish speakers, mostly in Roxbury. It and other organizations were doing the kind of work Frieda thought was important to fill the community's need. She advised the Roxbury Multi-Service Center how to support and strengthen such efforts, including helping La Alianza Hispana incorporate and expand its funding. In 1971, Frieda was named director of the alliance.

The Model Cities Program, part of President Lyndon Johnson's War on Poverty, was running strong, and Boston, like other cities, was receiving federal funding. Frieda persuaded the mayor and the city council to allocate a portion of its funding to La Alianza Hispana. "I never liked public speaking," she said, "but you do it if you have to. I went before the city council—it still amazes me that I did that—and fought and ended up being able to create a multiservice agency. We got a building. We got the whole thing."

ILLUS. 6.3   Frieda Garcia and Mayor Kevin White, 1974.
Photograph courtesy of Northeastern University Archives and
Special Collections, the La Alianza Hispana records.

At the 1974 groundbreaking, Frieda and Boston mayor Kevin
White greeted each other warmly. She had been in Boston only
nine years but already was a master negotiator at city hall and
a bridge builder among communities.

That same year, Frieda was invited to be a Community Fellow
at MIT. Mel King, a prominent Roxbury-based activist, had
started the program where participants studied urban issues,
honed their skills, and expanded their networks, and Hubie
Jones was the new director.

While digging into this period in Boston's history, I came
across a guest list for a dinner held in June 1974 at Boston's Parker
House Hotel. It illustrates the astounding range of connections
Frieda was making, even at that early stage of her career. Henry
Steele Commager, constitutional and intellectual historian from
Amherst College, was the dinner speaker. Journalist Bill Moyers
made the introduction, and around the table sat a select group of
the powerful and the up-and-coming: Congressman Tip O'Neil,

only a few years away from becoming speaker of the House; Vermont lawyer Patrick Leahy, then making his first bid for a U.S. Senate seat; chief aide to Massachusetts governor Frank Sargent; *Boston Globe* editor Thomas Winship and other political, corporate, and media personalities. Also Hubie Jones and Frieda.[7]

Soon, she was special assistant in Governor Sargent's administration to liaise with the Spanish-speaking community. She also worked at the Solomon Carter Fuller Mental Health Center. By this time, protests and violence against school busing were at their height, and Frieda was responsible for coordinating psychological counseling in the schools for students who were caught in the violence. In 1975, when Governor Michael Dukakis established the Judicial Nominating Commission, a nonpartisan group to screen candidates for state court positions, he designed it to include nonlawyer members of the community. At his invitation, Frieda became a member of the commission.

Let's step back and assess the wider landscape. By the 1970s, people were coming to realize that the world would not fall apart if women did things outside of tradition. Every time women like Dahlov Ipcar, Muriel Petioni, Cordelia Hood, Martha Lepow, Mildred Dresselhaus, and Frieda Garcia were successful, people around them grappled with the reality that women could do

ILLUS. 6.4   Frieda Garcia and Governor Michael Dukakis, undated. Photograph courtesy of Frieda Garcia.

more than expected. The grappling may have been begrudging, and some holdouts resisted enlightenment altogether, but when a patient was treated by a woman in a white coat, a defector was debriefed by someone in a skirt, a scientist with long hair made an important discovery, or a government official had his arm twisted by a woman wearing heels, it had the potential to put all women on the road to acceptance.

However, individual accomplishment, woman by woman, did not lead to widespread change. Beliefs about women's proper role were so ingrained that broader change could come only with upheaval. That upheaval began in the 1960s and continued into the 1970s.

The 1960s began with President Kennedy establishing the President's Commission on the Status of Women, which Eleanor Roosevelt, in one of her last official positions, chaired. The commission studied discrimination, including laws that excluded women from jury service, barred them from owning property or businesses, and kept them from legal control of their own earnings. The findings helped illuminate some of the evident disparities between men and women.[8]

Also in the 1960s, the movements for civil rights, Black power, and women's rights pushed the country further. Civil rights and Black power leaders were not necessarily focused on women's issues, but their rhetoric about equality was compelling. Racial minorities and women applied all the clout they could muster to convince the president, Congress, and the courts that it was time to change how Americans worked, traveled, and voted and where they could live. When Congress passed the Equal Pay Act of 1963, the Civil Rights Act of 1964, the Voting Rights Act of 1965, and the Equal Credit Opportunity Act of 1974, the courts had for the first time a statutory basis for deciding that discrimination on the basis of race, color, religion, national origin, or sex was no longer permissible. What that really meant would play out in the 1970s and later. It's still playing out today. But with these changes, women gained a new and growing presence in jobs that previously had been reserved for men.

There are two important side notes. One is a point that Jim Tankersley makes in his book *The Riches of This Land*. He writes that the 1964 Civil Rights Act had the effect of supercharging the growth of the middle class. Expanding opportunities for minorities and women created an upward flow of talent. More people were able to join the ranks of the middle class, which made the country as a whole better off.[9] The second thing to note is that women in secretarial and clerical jobs also spoke up. A group like 9to5, which started in Boston and spread across the country, gave women office workers a forum for obtaining pay equity and better working conditions, even before it inspired the movie starring Jane Fonda, Lily Tomlin, and Dolly Parton.[10]

Also of note is the fact that for generations, Black and brown women in Boston had been activists. In the twentieth century alone, there was Melnea Cass, a member of the NAACP who organized African American voters; was president of a women's service club; and, in 1949, joined with Muriel Snowden and her husband, Otto Snowden, to found Freedom House, a center for civil rights activism. Muriel Snowden's legacy continues to this day, with a city high school named for her. In the 1950s and 1960s, Ruth Batson challenged discrimination in public schools and later founded a program to bus city students to suburban schools. Her contemporary Elma Lewis opened an art school, a theater program, and an arts center, all to celebrate the work of African American artists. In 1973, Doris Bunte was elected to the state legislature as the first Black woman representative and later advanced the cause of integrated public housing as director of the Boston Housing Authority. This is only a cursory list, but the point is that Frieda worked in an environment where Black and brown women were clearly prominent.

Fewer women of Asian descent occupied similar positions, largely because the Chinese Exclusion Act had so effectively curbed immigration from China. One exception is Helen Chin Schlichte. Helen had a career in Massachusetts state government, beginning as a clerk in the State House and ending in the Executive Office of Administration and Finance. Like Frieda, she also played an outsized role in the nonprofit community.

Her story starts with her parents, both from Toishan village on China's south central coast. When he was fifteen, her father emigrated to the Charlestown neighborhood of Boston, home to a mostly Irish population, to join his father's laundry business, one of the few occupations a Chinese immigrant could hope for.

Some years later, Helen's mother arrived in Charlestown as a bride. She worked in the laundry while also raising a family. When Helen was fifteen, and the youngest of her eight siblings was three months old, her father died. The laundry business continued with her mother in charge and all the children assisting.

Her mother gave three pieces of advice that became the family's mantra: don't waste time, work a little harder, save your money. A fourth component was about the importance of education, and that sunk in too. All the children went to college, and Helen earned a graduate degree from Boston University.

When she was working in the administration and finance office, the state was sued for discriminatory hiring practices. Helen became the one to see that changes required by the court were implemented. "I am very precise," she told me. "I was always ready when we had to go see the judge." The judge, in turn, was so impressed that he praised the progress made under her watch in one of his written decisions.[11]

When I met Helen, she gave me a book her husband, George Schlichte, had written.[12] She had met him briefly when she was a teenager, scooping ice cream at a neighborhood pharmacy, but he had become a Catholic priest, and they lost touch. But they encountered one another again when he was leaving the priesthood and called the state Board of Higher Education with an inquiry. She, then assistant to the chancellor, answered the phone. After taking care of his inquiry, she invited him to lunch. "How about the Ritz?" she said. They met in the lobby of the grand hotel, and "she led the way up the wide carpeted marble stairs to the dining room. The maître d' greeted her like returning royalty." George was smitten. Once married, they became very involved with numerous charitable organizations.

Helen was on the board of Beth Israel Deaconness Medical Center, the Museum of Science, United Way of Massachusetts Bay, WGBH, the USS *Constitution* Museum, the Bostonian Society, the Boys and Girls Clubs of Boston, the Rose Fitzgerald Kennedy Greenway Conservancy, Boy Scouts, the Center for Women in Politics and Public Policy at the University of Massachusetts at Boston, and Kwong Kow Chinese School. George always said "give your money now while you're alive so you can see it working," and that's the principle on which they acted. Helen was also proud of being a cofounder of the South Cove Manor Nursing and Rehabilitation Center for elderly Asians. "I wanted to help my people," she said.

Perceptions about Asian women changed because of Helen and others. No longer were they deemed qualified to work only in a laundry, or perhaps a restaurant. Instead, they were more than qualified to work with the governor and help shape some of Boston's largest nonprofits. Also like Frieda, Helen bridged some of the divides that for generations had kept ethnic groups apart.

Meanwhile, Frieda's marriage to Timothy had come apart. At a demonstration against the Vietnam War, she met Byron Rushing, a man with an impressive résumé of community work at the Congress of Racial Equality and the Urban League. They are together today, more than forty years later.

I asked Frieda why this relationship had worked so well when her two marriages had failed. She paused for a moment before answering. "When I think about why the marriages failed and this relationship hasn't, I look at what the men did with their lives. In the case of John, nothing except have children. In the case of Timothy, his major claim to fame is that he made a documentary film on the tearing down of the elevated rail line in Boston. There wasn't the drive or the energy."

Byron has a great deal of both. In addition to his organizing work, he was president of Boston's Museum of African American History; a leader in the Episcopal Church; and, beginning in 1982, served thirty-six years in the state legislature, where he was known for speaking up on issues of civil rights, economic development, housing, and health care. He also was an early advocate for same-sex marriage, even though other religious leaders opposed it. In the Episcopal Church, he is a member of the House of Deputies, a founding member of the Episcopal Urban Caucus, and a board member of several church-affiliated organizations.

Might she get married? I dared to ask. "No need to change anything," she said. "We've been together forty-two years. He's an interesting man, always doing something. His daughter has given us two grandchildren, and we don't need to change a thing."

In 1981, Frieda became executive director of United South End Settlements (USES), a social service agency that consolidated

ILLUS. 6.5 Frieda Garcia and her family, undated. Photograph courtesy of her son-in-law Phillip Lartigue.

several of the city's original settlement houses. She explained the concept behind the settlement house movement. "It started in England, and the idea was something like what the Peace Corps was later. Young people, rich ones, went into poor parts of the city and lived and worked there for a time. The goal was to learn about poverty, not just to tell people what to do. Living together was the core of it, and it was a very good model."

By the time she was head of USES, the original model had evolved. The affluent no longer lived among the poor; instead, they were on the board of directors. "My board was fantastic," she said. "Some of them were old-line Bostonians from Beacon Hill, and they were the second or third generation of people in their families to serve on the board. They were deeply committed, and through them, I was able to meet other people involved in the power structure of Boston."

Frieda was comfortable working in ethnically and racially mixed terrain, but it could be tricky. In the case of USES, the board was mostly white, the clientele was mostly Black, and having a Latina director disappointed some. Frieda explained, "The runner-up for the director job was a Black male, and there were some people in the community who thought I should not have been hired at all. It was considered a Black agency and should have a Black person running it, but we just kept moving. I had to earn their respect. Mostly I did, but a few never came around."

In her twenty years with USES, Frieda faced an evolving set of challenges. As generous as many board members were, the organization needed additional funding. She organized a capital campaign, and its success meant that the Children's Art Center reopened; Camp Hale, a summer program in New Hampshire, continued operating; and new programs were added at headquarters. She also led a strategic planning process to keep pace with residential trends, economic development, and technology. She made a personal commitment to support other organizations that were trying to maintain affordable housing in the South End.

It is hard to overstate Frieda's clout among the city's philanthropic organizations. Over the years, she was on close to eighty nonprofit boards, including the Boston Foundation (which she chaired), the Isabella Stewart Gardner Museum, the United Way, the Red Cross, Boston Center for the Arts, the Massachusetts Foundation for the Humanities, the YWCA, Northeastern University, the Episcopal City Mission, the Massachusetts Women's Political Caucus, Associated Day Care, the Committee for Boston Public Housing, and Travelers Aid.

Many of these are boards where few are asked to serve, and most are invited because of their corporate position or financial means. Frieda had neither. But she did have skill in building coalitions. Her personality is upbeat and gregarious, and people were willing to listen to her, even if they started off skeptical. She had learned to balance budgets, run meetings, oversee staff, and raise money. She knew city and state leaders, and they knew her.

"This whole thing was stretching me like crazy," she said. "I was a woman, a minority person, and I was getting put on boards. When the United Way realized they had never had a woman on the executive committee, I got appointed to that. Some of the boards were just window dressing, but not all of them. And the thing is, I was learning about the power structure of Boston. It was like getting a degree in sociology and business combined."

The second time I met Frieda, we had lunch at a Puerto Rican restaurant. I got there first and took a small table near the door. When she arrived, she gave me a broad smile and signaled that I should follow her to a big round table in the corner. "This is my office," she laughed, putting down her bag.

She was dressed in a black turtleneck sweater, large gold hoop earrings, and a head wrap in a bold print fabric. She ordered for us both, speaking with the waiter in Spanish. She wanted me to try the house specialties: medianoche, a kind of sandwich, and plantain soup, served with crisp, fried slices of yucca. Then she fired questions at me. Where did I grow up? What was my son doing? Had I watched the presidential debate the night before, and what did I think of Donald Trump and Hillary Clinton? (This was 2016.) We talked about movies—she had just seen Joan Allen in the movie *Room* and thought I would like it too.

I mentioned the park named for her, but she confessed to being more proud of a different one. The Harriet Tubman Park had been neglected by the city for years, and Frieda had worked to refurbish it. Honoring a woman who risked her life to help others find freedom was, by itself, enough for this to be a pet project. But beyond that, Harriet Tubman had visited Boston both before and after the Civil War, to advocate for the abolition of slavery and to raise funds to support those whom she had led to freedom. One of the city's historic settlement houses, which was eventually consolidated into USES, was named for her.

The sculpture in the park shows Tubman with arm outstretched, leading five African Americans to freedom. Installed in 1999, it was the first sculpture on city property to pay tribute to a woman. The second sculpture in the park commemorates the signing of the Emancipation Proclamation. I can understand why this park is close to Frieda's heart. "The Harriet Tubman Park," she said, "was the most extraordinary thing I've done in my life, and it continues to be that."[13]

Over lunch, we also talked about mothers. "When I think about my mother now, I realize she had more strength than I realized at the time," Frieda said. "She was not as pampered as her younger sisters. When she was young, her father was just starting out, and his income was not as high as it later was. As a girl, she was not taught much of anything other than piano and sewing. But there she was with two children, living in Manhattan. What she did was very much outside the culture she grew up in."

So ironic—a mother preaching traditional values to her daughter while removing herself from them. I also heard a note of regret. "Talking to you," she said, "has reminded me that I had this pretty incredible example. As I now realize, I should have asked my mother a hell of a lot more questions. You think about the questions afterwards." How true.

Intermezzo
Another Part of the Story

When I told people that I went to law school because of my father, I spoke the truth, but selectively. My pat answer left out a big part of the story, which is my mother. I took too much about her for granted. Of course she ran things smoothly at home. Of course she cooked meals. Of course she took us wherever we needed to go after school. As far as I knew, that's what a mother did. But she had a life before and after that, not always centered on her family.

In the 1940s, my mother was an IBM "systems service girl." If you look at the company website today, you will see that IBM refers to the position as "systems service representative"; my mother, however, said it was "girl." Title aside, IBM was actually quite forward looking when it began to hire women to assist the sales force. As early as the 1930s, women would visit customer offices, assess their needs, and, once the new equipment was in place, train personnel on the latest equipment, such as punch card tabulators, calculators, and electric typewriters.

My mother began her tenure in upstate New York, near corporate headquarters, where she learned to use the equipment and studied business concepts so she would understand the environment where the machines would be used. When she had questions, she asked her father. "Dear Daddy," she wrote in one letter. "My understanding of 'Lead Time' is as follows," and then listed a series of questions about purchase forecasts, standing orders, volume, and discounts. She concluded with this: "Any other information you have on this subject will be greatly appreciated. Believe me." Then she added a postscript. "How do you like this proportional spacing machine? It's really the last word in typewriters. The mistakes are all mine." Her letter sits in front of me as I write this. She was right. Her letter does look sleeker, with proportional spacing.

She was asking the right person. My grandfather was purchasing manager of the Saco-Lowell Shops, a textile mill and manufacturing plant in Biddeford, Maine. He wrote back to explain the forecasting of material needs and a production schedule.

When the training course was complete, Mom went on the road. She traveled, met people, and earned a salary. Years later, when she told me about her job, her enthusiasm was still palpable. She used to boast that she earned more than Dad did in his first job as a lawyer. But she wanted desperately to be a mother, and when she was pregnant with me, she left her job. Unlike some of the women in this book, she could not imagine keeping her job while also being a mother.

She never showed regret about her decision, even when her three kids drove her crazy, as I know we did. But, with a child's cunning, I would ask whether she missed her job. Sometimes I felt a hint of something else, as though she might be contemplating the path not taken, but she never let any regret show.

When my brother, the youngest, was in high school, Mom went back to work. This was the mid-1970s, the very time that Frieda Garcia was becoming known as an activist in Boston. Only a few miles apart, their lives were very different, but both were in the business of helping others. My mother and a business partner started a placement agency to help women find jobs. Her typical client was a suburban woman who had been out of the job market for years. Some were getting divorced and needed money; others, with grown kids, wanted something to do. Mom helped them craft a résumé. She urged them to list all their volunteer activities and assured them that an employer would see their value. She put them through mock interviews and coached them on better answers. She networked with businesses and found job openings. She gave her clients the confidence they needed to adapt to their changed circumstances.

I started this book after my mother died. While I was writing, a friend of hers sent me a yellowed newspaper clipping. Dated 1980, it had run in the *Needham Chronicle,* a suburban weekly that no longer exists. The subject was Women West, a network for professional and businesswomen that my mother had started after she went back to work in the 1970s. The article featured a black-and-white photograph of my mother seated at a desk, phone receiver at her ear, pen in hand. The caption reads, "Women's networks—where the power is."

The article came out just a few months before I graduated from law school. I was caught up in final exams, worrying about the bar exam I would take that summer, and not paying much attention to my mother.

She is quoted in the article. Here she is explaining the goal of her organization. "The monthly meetings bring professional women together to exchange information, to socialize and to help them achieve their personal career goals through a sharing of resources. There is a bonding in women's networks, like the bonding men have traditionally enjoyed on the squash court or in men's clubs."

When I showed the article to my husband, he said, "You are just like your mother." This surprised me. I understood I was like my father, but my husband saw a connection that I, so used to thinking I had followed my father's path, failed to see.

In 1974, a small group of women who were executives at banks in Boston saw their male colleagues leave the office every day at noon. The men went to private clubs for lunch, where they talked, created a network, and made business referrals. On their way out of the office, they walked past the few women who were, for the first time, their executive colleagues. If it occurred to any of the men to invite a woman to join him, he could not, because women were barred from men's clubs, except on very special occasions.

Four women instead met for lunch at a downtown restaurant. They wanted to make friends and build their own network. From that very modest beginning, the Boston Club, the group they started, grew to more than six hundred members. Several years before I received the yellowed clipping in the mail, I was president of the Boston Club. It's a bigger version of Women West, doing what my mother wanted her organization to do—help women achieve their career goals through a sharing of resources. Long after the fact, and helped by my husband's insight, I saw that I had indeed followed in my mother's footsteps.

The Second Wave Rises
Rya Weickert Zobel, Federal Judge
(b. 1931)

The last interview I conducted for this book was with Rya Zobel, a judge on the U.S. District Court in Boston. I knew who she was before we met. Ten years earlier, I had litigated a case in her courtroom. Opposing counsel and I argued several legal motions and had a series of conferences with the judge. I saw enough of her in action to know she was confident and business-like. I also knew, from my own clerkship with a federal judge, that a judge who is business-like in the courtroom may show a different side in private. So it was with Judge Zobel. In chambers, she was relaxed and funny. She wore black slacks, a white blouse, and a boldly patterned red jacket, easy to slip off if she had to don the black robe for an emergency hearing.

Before we met, I tried to gather background information, but surprisingly little was available. Basic facts were on the court website—date of birth, schools attended, date sworn in as a judge. Also, I knew who her ex-husband was: I once had a case before him in the Massachusetts Superior Court. But more in-depth facts were sparse. It seemed she had not given many interviews, and those she had given had produced generalities for the most part.

Obviously, I wanted to interview a lawyer. Imagining the lives of women lawyers had started me on this quest in the first place. I had tried but failed to track down the women in my father's yearbook. Probably some had changed their names with marriage and some had retired or died by the time I looked for them. I asked, but the Yale alumni office was unable to help.

So I was lucky that a friend who once was Judge Zobel's law clerk was willing to make an email introduction. I took it from there, and in my first phone call with the judge, she signaled her resistance to my idea. "I never was ambitious," she said. This confounded me. As a federal judge, she occupied a top echelon of the profession. No one just walks into that job. She had to have had oomph of some kind. But there I was, primed for the final interview in my exploration of female ambition, and she was rejecting the paradigm.

Virginia Woolf once wrote an essay that serves as a warning to biographers. In the desire to create a significant life story, she wrote, biographers attach meaning to their subjects' actions and words that the subjects themselves never conceived. Was I wrong to think Judge Zobel's life involved ambition when she said it didn't? Was I dragging along a preconceived notion that did not fit? I kept Virginia Woolf in mind, but I plunged ahead knowing, at the very least, that Rya Zobel was exceptional.[1]

She had to be exceptional, because the legal field was so resistant to change. For more than a century, women angled for the right to represent clients. Often, when they did become members of the bar, they were excluded from the courtroom. Compared to medicine, law was far more restrictive.

It did not start out that way. In the middle of the nineteenth century, the first women doctors and first women lawyers started working at about the same time. Elizabeth Blackwell, her sister Emily Blackwell, and Mary Putnam Jacobi became doctors in 1849, 1854, and 1864, respectively, only a few years before Arabella Mansfield was admitted, in 1869, to the Iowa bar. But after these "firsts," things took a turn.

In 1870, for example, Myra Bradwell passed the qualifying exam in Illinois, but when she applied to become a member of the bar, the state turned her down because she was married.[2]

She nevertheless persisted and took her case to the U.S. Supreme Court. There she lost again, and in the 1873 case of *Bradwell v. Illinois*, Justice Joseph Bradley took it upon himself to explain that no woman should have a career of any sort, because that was the divine order. Here is an excerpt from his concurring opinion:

> The natural and proper timidity and delicacy which belongs to the female sex evidently unfits it for many of the occupations of civil life. The constitution of the family organization, which is founded in the divine ordinance, as well as in the nature of things, indicates the domestic sphere as that which properly belongs to the domain and functions of womanhood. The harmony, not to say identity, of interest and views which belong, or should belong, to the family institution is repugnant to the idea of a woman adopting a distinct and independent career from that of her husband. . . . The paramount destiny and mission of woman are to fulfill the noble and benign offices of wife and mother. This is the law of the Creator.[3]

Sometimes women wrangled a partial concession from the court. For instance, one judge opined that women could engage in activities outside the home, as long as they stayed away from law. Case in point: Lavinia Goodell, the first woman licensed to practice law in Wisconsin, had a client whose case was pending before the state supreme court. When she sought permission to argue the case, the court, in an 1875 opinion, said no:

> There are many employments in life not unfit for female character. The profession of the law is surely not one of these. The peculiar qualities of womanhood, its gentle graces, its quick sensibility, its tender susceptibility, its purity, its delicacy, its emotional impulses, its subordination of hard reason to sympathetic feeling, are surely not qualifications for forensic strife.[4]

The court's use of double negatives does not mask the point that women were just too feminine for law.

In her study of professional women in the Progressive Era, which ran from approximately 1890 to 1920, historian Joyce Antler explained the consequences of society's view of women's inherent feminine nature. In medicine, caring for others was part of the profession, which meant that women could eke out a place. Even if they did not excel in the hard sciences, they could render comfort at the patient's bedside. There was no parallel in law. Business and real estate were fundamental to the practice of law. Women, being as delicate as they were, did not know anything about these subjects and were too emotional to learn. Professor Antler summed it up this way:

> Unlike the profession of medicine, where women's supposed nurturant qualities afforded them a special place, the practice of law seemed to require no peculiarly feminine qualities. On the contrary, many female attorneys themselves noted the close connection between law, masculine habits of thought and work, and the characteristics of industrial civilization. The primary concern of the law with property and the values of the business world led many observers to believe that females were particularly unsuited to its demands.[5]

When the Progressive Era wound down in 1920, women composed 5 percent of the country's doctors but only 1 percent of its lawyers. From that perspective, you could say that medicine was five times more hospitable to women.[6]

It took a century for law to catch up. Today, about one-third of practitioners in both fields are women. But in 1956, when Rya graduated from Harvard Law School, the evolution to where we are today was only about one-third complete.[7]

Rya's class at Harvard was only the fourth with any women. Since 1871, women had petitioned for admission to the law school, but not until 1949 did the faculty agree to admit them, and then only a trickle. Once women were in the door, some professors refused to call on them, even though a hallmark of the Socratic method used at most law schools, including Harvard,

ILLUS. 7.1 Rya Zobel and Judith Cowin, associate justice of the Massachusetts Supreme Judicial Court (ret.), 2010. Photograph taken at an event sponsored by the Commonwealth Shakespeare Company.

which pioneered it, is for professors and students to engage in open dialogue about the reasoning behind a court decision. Maybe professors wanted to protect women from the surprise of being called on or shield them from having to display their "inferior" intellectual or verbal skills.[8]

Some professors set aside one day each term as Ladies' Day, when women knew they would be called on. Some women thought Ladies' Day was proof of ongoing discrimination. Rya brushed it off entirely. "I just liked learning," she said.[9]

At graduation, Rya could not land a job with a law firm. "Law firms were not hiring girls," she said. "And we were not women. We were 'girls.'" Men had returned to civilian life, meaning more than enough male lawyers were eager to fill law firm openings. Of the few women who did work at firms, most were associates, not partners, and generally in practice areas like trusts and estates. Very rarely were they doing corporate deals or litigating in the courtroom, where deadlines were pressing, confrontation was the norm, and, significantly, they would have more opportunity to generate revenue. (Revenue generation is always a factor when a firm decides who will become a partner.)[10]

Government service was an alternative, and Rya became a law clerk to Judge George Sweeney of the federal district court in Boston. For a young lawyer, there is nothing like working closely with a judge. You see how cases are run in the courtroom. In chambers, you talk through the legal issues on which a case turns and draft opinions. You see areas of law, criminal, for instance, you might miss in private practice. Typically, a clerkship lasts a year or two, but Rya stayed with Judge Sweeney for ten.

It was a good time for her to have that job. She was married to a man she had met in college, and they had three adopted children. With the clerkship, she had more predictability in her schedule than if she were with a firm. Being home for dinner with the children was a real perk. This sounds like a dream job for any American woman with children, but Rya grew up far from an American dream.

She was born in Zwickau, Germany, a small industrial city near Dresden. Although it was a center for automobile manufacturing, her family had nothing to do with that. Her father managed a fine art print shop that produced calendars and cards. Her mother was a violinist who played with a group of local musicians. In spirit, they were closer to Robert Schumann, the Romantic period composer, also born in Zwickau, than to modern manufacturing.

In 1933, when Rya was two, Adolf Hitler became German chancellor. Her parents saw troubling signs, particularly since Rya's mother was Jewish. She had been born in Hungary, and two of her brothers were already in the United States. "My uncles," Rya said, "came in the late twenties because they understood full well that, as Jews, they had no opportunities in Hungary. Uncle Steve tried for a long time to get us to come here. But my parents, particularly my father, didn't really want to leave."

Her parents continued debating whether to go or stay, but by the time they decided to go, Germany was at war, and it was too late. Rya's mother did manage to get falsified papers from Hungary that expunged her Jewishness, and the family stayed in Zwickau, where her mother's religious background was kept secret, even from the children.

Most of the war years included going to school. "We went to school until December of '44, and then school stopped. I didn't go to school again until January of '47, when I came here," Rya said. War also meant dodging bombs. "There was one occasion where the planes were coming so low that they actually shattered the house. We were in the basement, and the planes went over with machine guns. The attic was the place where during bad weather laundry was hung to dry. When it was over there were all these sheets with holes in them. It was really funny in a way."

By the end of the war, Germany was devastated. Millions of uprooted people were living in camps; millions more were dead. Roads and railway tracks were impassable. The country had no working currency and little food. Allied forces occupied the country, split into four zones. Initially, the Americans had control of Zwickau, but they turned it over to the Soviets, it being in the eastern part of the country. Rya's parents were optimistic. "My parents didn't leave because they thought they had nothing to fear from the Russians. My mother was sort of pleased that they had come because they had a reputation of being very good with artists"—a reputation that meant nothing in occupied Germany, as it turned out.

"Apparently there was some teenage boy in the neighborhood who, for some reason, didn't like us," she continued. "He told the Russians that my parents were spies for the Americans. One day in July of '45, a bunch of Russian officers came to the house. They told my brother and me to go outside, which we did. Fortunately, it was a nice day. A couple of them came back with my father, took him inside for a while, and then brought him out. As he was leaving, my father told me to take care of my mother and my brother. I never saw him again.

"Later in the day, the Russians came back for my mother. They said she will be back soon, but she wasn't. I was thirteen, my brother was ten, and we were suddenly without parents."

The emotional impact was enormous. For much of her life, Rya could not dwell on it. "I have not been able to reconstruct the days after my parents were taken away. All of this, I never really processed until recently when Trump started separating families, and suddenly it occurred to me that that's what happened to us." (Rya said this during an interview in September 2019.)

The couple who owned the print shop where her father had worked lived upstairs. They arranged for Rya and her brother to leave Zwickau and live on a farm in a nearby village, where food was more likely to be found, even though food was scarce everywhere. On the farm, Rya remembered, she had to lug buckets of water back to the farmhouse. Still, being there was better than remaining in their house with neither parents nor food.

Relatives in Coburg, just west of the line that divided the Soviet and American sectors, were beyond Rya's reach. "There was no communication between the east and the west," she said. "No telephone. No nothing. But at some point, my aunt, my father's sister who lived in Coburg, in the west, sent a messenger to find out what had happened to us. The messenger reported back and then was told to bring us out."

In the fall, the messenger returned to escort Rya and her brother to Coburg, roughly a hundred miles away. "It took us something like three or four days to get to the border. We traveled by train, in *Viehwagen,* cattle cars. At the Holocaust Museum in Washington, there is such a car. And you know—it was very emotional to me because I went to freedom in such a car, just like the ones that took other people to their deaths."

Arriving at the border, they found it patrolled on both sides. The Soviets wanted to keep able-bodied workers inside their zone, and the Americans were trying to limit the many thousands trying to flee west.[11]

"When we finally got to the border, all the trees had been cut so the guards could see people traveling. There were watch towers, and there was barbed wire, which did a certain amount of damage to a cape I was wearing." Rya chuckled, remembering the torn cape.

"We arrived early in the morning, four or five o'clock, just as the milk wagons were going into town. We hitched a ride on a milk wagon into the town of Coburg, just on the other side of the border, where we went to live with my aunt and her husband."

For months, Rya had operated on a basic instinct for

survival—food, water, and shelter. Once in Coburg, she allowed herself to think, at least a little, about what she wanted.

"My uncle always wanted a son, and he had a good relationship with my brother. He was not very understanding of women and girls, and I had lots of run-ins with him. He wanted me to be a servant, and I wasn't cut out for that. My aunt had a friend, a lovely woman who kept giving me books to read. One day, when I was supposed to be doing chores, I wanted to finish what I was reading. My uncle took the book and burned it. Put it right into the fireplace."

Eventually, her uncle Steve arrived from the United States to see about his sister's children. At this point, Rya broke the narrative and asked me a question: "Do you know what the definition of a Hungarian is?"

It happened that I did know a definition, one I had heard from my husband's Austrian family with their own Hungarian relatives, but I waited to hear if hers would match mine. "It's the guy who goes into the revolving door behind you and comes out in front of you." I laughed—it was exactly the same definition. "That was Uncle Steve," she said.

Two children stranded in a devastated Europe without parents, a Hungarian uncle who knew how to get things done, one way or another—he was exactly who they needed.

"Steve asked whether we wanted to come to the United States. My brother said no. I said yes." She prevailed.

By this time, the United Nations Relief and Rehabilitation Administration (UNRRA) was working with the occupation forces to handle the millions of displaced persons and refugees. The scale of need was enormous, and several months passed before the correct permits were issued. At one point while the children were waiting, Steve came back to Coburg to check on them and brought Rya a valuable gift: cigarettes. Teachers in displaced persons camps were being paid in cigarettes. In Berlin, American soldiers were making serious money selling their tobacco allotments. But Rya, still a girl, did not know how to trade on the black market. "I had a big bunch of cigarettes," she said, "which were the coin of the realm, but I didn't know how to deal with them, so I gave them away."[12]

Finally, in late 1946, it was time to leave Coburg. "We went to Munich for two or three or four weeks. I remember that we slept in bunk rooms and the mattresses were literally straw. My brother and I shared a bed, wearing full clothing, and finally our paperwork was okayed. Somehow we got to Bremen and waited for the ship. When the ship showed up, it was the SS *Ernie Pyle,* named for the war correspondent."[13]

Rya was fifteen and leaving behind the only country she knew—the place where she knew the language, had gone to school, and had last seen her parents. She had no way to predict what life would be like in a new country, but she was optimistic.

"On the Atlantic, there was a big storm," she remembered. "The crossing took thirteen days, and I was sick the whole time. But when we sailed into New York Harbor, in front of the Statue of Liberty, everyone came on deck, including all those who had been sick, and we all cheered."

Now, as a federal judge, Rya holds naturalization ceremonies. It is an uplifting part of the job, but she does regret one thing. "Nobody anymore gets to have the great privilege of arriving in New York Harbor and seeing the Statue of Liberty. It was an amazing experience."

Her two uncles, Steve and his brother Andy, met Rya and her brother at the dock, accompanied by their wives and Rya's grandmother. Together with the other children from the ship, they all took a bus to the Bronx for processing at a UNRRA facility. Rya could not believe her eyes. "Here were these twenty-one or twenty-two children who had lived through deprivations, you know, darkened windows and no food available. We drove up Broadway, and in front of all the stores the food was spilling out onto the street. There were baskets, and box after box of fruit that we hadn't seen. Ever. We were oohing and aahing, and the bus driver kept saying, 'Everybody happy? Everybody happy?' It was really quite a wonderful experience. And after dinner, my relatives took us out for a banana split. My first. Ever.

"The next morning, we took the subway to my grandmother's apartment on Riverside Drive. I learned about *Uptoven* and *Doventoven,* 'uptown' and 'downtown' in German. From there we drove to Sea Cliff, where we moved in with my uncle Andy and his family."

Andy and his wife, Patty, lived in a modest house near the

water in Sea Cliff, on the north shore of Long Island. They had two teenagers and an eighteen-month-old, and now two more teenagers. "To take us in and feed us, to clothe us, to educate us—it was a remarkable family."

Within a week, Rya and her brother were in the local school. They knew a little English but had a lot of catching up to do. At home, they had to speak English, even though Andy and Patty also knew German. "I remember coming home from school with a headache every day for weeks, because it required so much concentration," Rya said. "But it was a good thing to do. They were right to do it this way."

Within two and a half years at the local high school, Rya was ready for college, which was definitely part of the family's plan. Her first choice was Cornell, but when she was turned down, Susanne Langer, a family friend who had grown up in New York's German émigré community, suggested Radcliffe, where she taught philosophy. That worked out, and Rya started Radcliffe in the fall of 1949.

She liked her classes, but she really liked the social life. "I had wonderful friends who were my roommates. I had lots of dates, which was important at the time. And I liked the jolly-ups," the name for Radcliffe dances with men from Harvard and MIT. On nights when she did not have a date, Rya watched her friends come home from theirs. "In my first year, my room was right over the front door and I could watch people come and go. We had to be in by ten at night, eleven on weekends."

In sophomore year, she got a part-time job restacking books in the library. By her junior year, she was working as a research assistant for a professor in the government department, even though she was an economics major. "He encouraged me to go to law school," she said. "He did that to every student he liked. I didn't have any particular ambition at the time. I wasn't really sure I wanted to go to law school, and I put it off." When she finally decided she would apply, "it was so late that literally I had to send the application for taking the LSAT by special mail delivery. When I applied to Harvard Law School, it was the fourth class to include women."[14]

Being one of a handful of women did not faze her. Other things were more challenging—constitutional law, for instance.

ILLUS. 7.2   Rya Zobel, undated. Photograph courtesy of Rya Zobel.

"I really didn't know enough American history. It wasn't part of me. It was like learning something totally new. I didn't have that same sense that this is who we are that an American student would normally have."

The language also tripped her up, not English per se, but some of the legal terminology. "In property class, we learned how property was handed down in England," she said. "Because of primogeniture, everything went to the oldest son. The girls, of course, never got anything. There were what the professor called 'uses,' a particular kind of title. There were 'shifting uses' and 'springing uses,' depending on how title passed to the boy. And because we were talking about young men who would be the owners, I misunderstood and thought it was y-o-u-t-h-s. I had this image of shifting youths and springing youths. That's what I wrote in my notes, and somewhere I still have my old notebooks. They're stored in my house in boxes from the Harvard Coop."

Occasionally a rumor about her parents would reach her: her father had had a stroke or had taken his own life. It was impossible to know what really happened. She knew only that he never came back after that July day. But in her second year of law school, a telegram arrived from Coburg. From her mother, it simply said, "I'm coming." They met at her grandmother's apartment on Riverside Drive, where her mother told her what had happened. Convicted of sabotage in a Soviet show trial, she was imprisoned, first in Siberia as a political prisoner, then in a prison for real criminals, where her life was on the line every day. Ten years into her sentence, her jailers asked where she wanted to go—east or west, a ludicrous question, given what East Germany had become. She went west to her relatives in Coburg, then to New York. The violinist who was once fleetingly optimistic about life under Soviet control now had other thoughts: "My mother used to say that Russians operate the system so that everybody sat, sits or will sit in prison. It's arbitrary, and it's nearly inevitable for most."

Rya reflected on her parents' different natures. Her more cautious father "was not easily moved from his accustomed place. I do not think he would have done well here. He was not the person my mother was, who was very adaptable. She made good."

When Judge Sweeney died ten years into her clerkship, Rya had to find a new job. She again looked at law firms, and now, in 1966, some were willing to hire a woman. She became an associate at Hill & Barlow, a mid-sized Boston firm, where she litigated divorce cases. This was a new area of the law for her, and it required an expertise in contract and tax law as well as courtroom technique. She mastered all that, but when the question of partnership arose, the firm said not now, maybe next year. Dissatisfied, she talked to a lawyer whom she knew from the courtroom, who said that his firm, Goodwin, Procter & Hoar, might be interested in hiring a good litigator. She switched firms and, in 1976, became her new firm's first woman partner.

Goodwin Proctor had made a point of hiring lawyers who were "firsts," beginning in the 1960s. With a Jewish, an African American, and a woman lawyer, the firm was already at the progressive end of the spectrum for Boston law firms. In 2012, the firm celebrated its centennial and prepared a book that recounted its history and the lawyers who had worked there over the years. About Rya, they wrote that she was hired because the firm's lawyers "admired her work while negotiating with her from the other side of the table." She had a lasting impact because "her outstanding performance served to destroy forever a previous stereotype that women lawyers were suitable *only* for probate, domestic relations or real estate law."[15]

I am conscious of the debt I owe to women like Rya for the example they set. In 1982, when I finished my clerkship with a federal judge in Connecticut, I practiced with a law firm in Hartford. Seven years later, I became a litigation partner, the fourth woman partner in the firm. Business, commercial, and tax cases were my bailiwick. In the courtroom, I was sometimes the only woman. But back in the office, I had the help of two other women litigators, one of whom is now also a federal trial judge. They set a high bar of accomplishment and were invariably encouraging to me.

In the mid-1980s, the firm announced that lawyers could work part-time. Predictably, this was of great interest to mothers of young children. One colleague advised me to get out of litigation so that I would be able to work part-time if I became a mother. If I wrote wills or counseled clients about employment disputes, she said, I would not have to go to court or meet the incessant deadlines of litigation.

My perspective was different. I was concerned that the part-time option would create a ghetto for women where they would lag behind men who billed more hours, generated more revenue, and become partners sooner. Also, I did not want to concede that we women had some inherent "female" quality that rendered us unqualified to handle the full range of legal work. I did not want to see women in any pigeonhole, particularly one they had been trying to escape since the nineteenth century. When I did become a mother, I worked full-time because I was single and the only source of income for my two-person household. I never did wrestle with the implications of that alternative work arrangement.

By the time Rya joined Goodwin Proctor, she was married to Hiller Zobel, her second husband, also a lawyer. He came with four stepchildren, two of whom, plus Rya's three, lived at their house in Cohasset, south of Boston. I asked Rya how she divided her time between work and family, even though I knew this question is almost never asked of men. "When the kids were young, we had a couple from Brazil take care of things at home. At some point, the kids were all in school and there wasn't enough childcare to keep both of them busy, so they bought a small house nearby and worked for other people. Except Eva still came to our house, to clean and be there when the kids came home from school, and maybe do some driving if they needed it. Every week I would order groceries by phone. On Saturday we would get a case of half gallon bottles of milk delivered, and by Wednesday it would be gone. I did most of the cooking on Sundays. Things like lasagnas and Hungarian stews. I don't know how I managed it."

In 1978, Congress authorized an expansion of the federal courts, giving President Jimmy Carter what was then an unprecedented opportunity to shape the judiciary. Carter vowed to increase the number of women and African American judges, even though James Eastland of Mississippi, an avowed segregationist, was the longtime chair of the Senate Judiciary Committee. But Eastland may have wanted to make Carter, his fellow southerner, look good, and he agreed to procedural changes that paved the way for the incoming committee chair, Senator Ted Kennedy of Massachusetts, to oversee confirmation hearings.[16]

"It was late 1978, the day after Thanksgiving, when Kennedy called me," Rya recalled. "I thought it was the grocery store calling. I had just left a message at the store about that week's delivery, and when the phone rang, I thought it was the store calling back. But no. It was Senator Kennedy. Four judgeships were allotted to Massachusetts, and it was very clear that there would be one Black and one woman in the group. David Nelson became the first Black judge, and I became the woman. My competition was not much. Ruth Abrams was approached, but she was on the state Supreme Judicial Court, and she didn't want to leave it. She would have been a shoo-in."[17]

Rya meant no disrespect when she said there was not much competition. She meant that very few women had the judicial, prosecutorial, or academic experience that would normally be a qualification. Almost no women were law school professors or deans. None was a district attorney, and they were scarce on the state court bench. In Massachusetts, a few women had broken ground as judges in the early years of the twentieth century, but those first forays were followed by decades with no women at all on the bench—or on juries; I was surprised to learn when I was called for jury service and watched the instructional video that women were not permitted to sit on a jury until 1951. Even then, Massachusetts was the only state where a woman could ask to be excused simply because of gender or if she thought the evidence or deliberations would be embarrassing.[18]

This graphic shows the gender breakdown of federal judges all the way back to 1789, when the federal court system began. For 140 years, it's all green, until a barely perceptible speck of blue appears in 1928, when Genevieve Rose Cline became a judge on the U.S. Customs Court. Two more women joined the federal judiciary in 1934 and 1949, and the speck becomes a little bigger. Only in 1979, with President Carter's appointments, do the dots become a thin blue line. Some people, of course, wanted Carter to do more, but what he did do was historic. Of 262 judges, 37 were Black, 16 were Hispanic, and 41 were female.[19]

In the Senate Judiciary Committee hearing, Rya got a softball question: how do you compare your experience as a federal law clerk to what a judgeship will be like? She told the senators that the caseload per federal judge had doubled since the time she

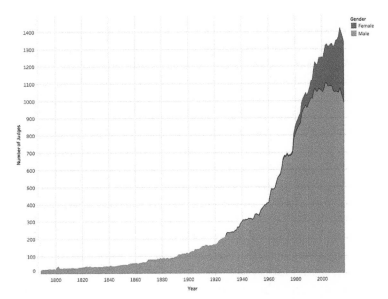

ILLUS. 7.3   Article III judges by gender, 1789–2017. From the Federal Judicial Center.

clerked, and judges had to be effective managers. A month later, she was sworn in at Faneuil Hall. For fourteen years, she was the only woman to serve on the federal court in Massachusetts.

For Rya, becoming a federal judge was not the result of burning ambition or strategic maneuvering to get on the bench. She made it seem as though it was simply the next logical step in her career. "I liked this court when I was here as a law clerk. And I thought I could do the work. It was intimidating in a way, but I was very familiar with the court, so it was much easier for me than it is for some people who come from the outside. I went back to the same building where I had clerked. I knew the surroundings and the personnel." She also liked the autonomy and the authority. "I did my own thing. I could do exactly what I wanted to do, the way I wanted to do it."

She became known for handling cases efficiently, as she told the Judiciary Committee she would—with early conferences, close monitoring of deadlines, and lots of communication with lawyers to keep a case on track—and also for applying a light touch to the part of the job where she had to keep courtroom order. On long trial days, she used breaks to lead jury members in yoga stretches.

The governor of Massachusetts, Bill Weld, asked her to join the state's highest court. "I decided I didn't want to do that. Another time I was asked to go to the Court of Appeals for the First Circuit. I decided not to do that. This is where I belong. It's interesting work, and you work with people. On appeals courts, they work with paper. Seriously, you can tell. When you read appellate opinions, sometimes you can tell they don't understand how things work in the courtroom."

One job she would have liked, but did not get, was attorney general. President Bill Clinton chose Janet Reno as the first woman for that job. But Rya did want a change, at least temporarily, because her marriage was disintegrating. Her husband, by then a state court judge, had taken up with another judge on the same court. When a reporter for the *Boston Globe* called the house to confirm the rumor, Rya answered. In what I imagine was her most tart voice, she told the reporter to ask her husband.[20] Given that all the participants were well known in legal circles, the divorce became fodder for gossip and speculation.

"I needed to get out of town," she said, and she took the opportunity to become director of the Federal Judicial Center in Washington, D.C. The center conducts research and runs programs to educate judges and court personnel on legal issues. Her particular focus, for the three years she was director, was using technology in the courtroom and examining inequities in criminal sentencing. Congress had passed guidelines, including mandatory minimum sentences, that led to unfairness in sentencing—the opposite of what the guidelines were supposed to achieve. "You know, it was impossible to use the guidelines fairly," she said. "The country is so big and diverse, its cultures are quite different. An offense in one place might be looked at differently somewhere else. The sentencing guidelines didn't distinguish." After a nationwide study, the center proposed changes that were a model for Congress when it later modified the guidelines.

I asked Rya what she thought a woman should do to be successful in law. Her answer came in two parts. One had to do with attitude. She described a lawsuit where a woman who wanted to open a massage business had sued her town's board of health after it refused to issue a business license. In the courtroom, the lawyers referred to the plaintiff as a "girl," even though she was in her twenties and had a child. Rya took a creative approach. "Finally, I said, 'Gentlemen, let's just stop here. You may refer to the plaintiff as a girl, and we will refer to the defendants on the board of health as boys.' And that's what they did."

She could have used other tools to enforce standards of behavior in her courtroom. She had the authority conveyed by her black robe, the gavel, and the power to impose sanctions. But she understood the wisdom of handling this situation with humor rather than pique. "Instead of brooding over their disrespect for women, I encouraged them in other ways. My sense is that these guys learned something. And they ended up making fun of themselves. I think one of the problems with the women's movement is there is no sense of humor, and sometimes a sense of humor helps."

Her second piece of advice had to do with practice areas—and here she sounded like Rosalyn Yalow talking to the young Mildred Dresselhaus. "Pick an area that is highly specialized and become good at it. Tax law, for instance. You don't practice in that area unless you're a specialist, but when you're good, you're in demand. Actually, any kind of specialty is a way for women to get ahead, particularly one that is not seen as a 'woman's place.' It could be patent law, intellectual property, or something else."

In her own career, she had done just that, going into litigation when most women did not. But it was not that she had picked an unusual area as a way to get ahead. Litigation just seemed interesting to her. "I think," she said, "the really lovely thing about litigation is that you get such a varied practice. You learn so many things." The same goes for being a trial judge. "I've learned so much about things that I would never even have thought about, if not for this job."

Recently, Rya was honored by the Federal Bar Association. She was amused as she listened to remarks about her, including the yoga stretches. But when the bar association presented her with a rocking chair, she was really pleased.

A coda to my interview came a year later, almost exactly to the day, when it was announced that Rya was being given the

ILLUS. 7.4 Judge Rya Zobel, 2019. Photograph courtesy of the Massachusetts Chapter of the Federal Bar Association.

ILLUS. 7.5 Judge Rya Zobel, in her awarded rocking chair, 2019. Photograph courtesy of the Massachusetts Chapter of the Federal Bar Association.

2020 Edward J. Devitt Distinguished Service to Justice Award, the highest award that can be given to a federal judge. Her fellow judges in Massachusetts nominated her, and their letter to the selection committee noted a litany of accomplishments, including her leadership on committees and her stint at the Federal Judicial Center. But what really stands out is their description of her as a person. "Rya Zobel *the person*," they wrote, "is what sets her apart from the rest as both a judge and a human being." They, younger judges on the court, learned from her that the courthouse was a place of collegiality. They wrote that she brings "a contagious zest to her work that infects all those around her with her delight in the judicial process, her openness to each new challenge, and her seriousness of purpose (but never excessive seriousness of self)."[21]

When Rya accepted the award, she had this to say about how she tries to do her job. "Judicial temperament is a lack of arrogance born of self-confidence, of a sense of self. It is an intuitive respect for all who appear before you. It is both measured restraint and measured intervention. It is fairness. It is equal treatment and open consideration of all participants in the process."[22]

In retrospect, Rya made me rethink what ambition means for women. She was right. She was not ambitious in the way we usually think of it. She did not set out to become a judge or even a lawyer, and once she was a lawyer, she did not maneuver her career to get on the bench.

She followed her intellectual interests. Even though women were not expected to excel in areas like economics and tax, she did, because that is what interested her. In the courtroom, where women were regarded as interlopers, she mastered its techniques and won converts. She did not oppose cultural norms so much as she ignored them. Maybe this is ambition in its purest form.

Epilogue

When I think of myself at eight years old, studying pictures in my father's yearbook, I have to laugh. Did I really think I would learn, from looking at a hairstyle or a necklace, why a woman went to law school? Also bonkers was my suspicion that a secret ingredient explained everything, if only I could discover it. Obviously, there is no one ingredient. Every woman lives a mosaic of experiences that meld in unique ways.

Even within one life, influences were inconsistent and paths winding. Yet, within the portraits I have drawn are repeating themes. In my head is a Venn diagram of the women's lives, with overlapping circles and clusters of experience.

The revelation that most surprised me is how many women came from families recently arrived to this country. Immigration colored the life of almost every woman in the book: Dahlov Ipcar's father from Lithuania, Muriel Petioni from Trinidad, Martha Lepow's and Mildred Dresselhaus's families from Russia and Poland, Frieda Garcia from the Dominican Republic, Rya Zobel from Germany. The only woman whose family arrived in this country more than a generation back was Cordelia Hood, and hers was a pioneer family.

I did not think about immigration, one way or the other, when I started this project. But now that I see the result, I have to ask, does immigration matter? Within our families, we all hear stories about where we came from and where we hope to go. We tell similar stories to our children, and they animate us. When we believe that we will be free to follow a "liberating profession," as Muriel Petioni's father hoped, it imparts a certain uplift to the immigration experience, even if reality is laced with discrimination. When the story is that we escaped religious pogroms, we cannot deny that immigration is a positive step, even if disappointments follow. The decision to come to a new country requires a sense of daring and exploration, and that, too, can become part of the family ethos. Couple that with education and see if it does not yield girls who are willing to make bold choices about their lives.

Religion was not part of my calculus, either, when I chose women to interview. In my meetings, I did not probe the subject, but it surfaced naturally in some of the conversations. When I mentioned to a friend that an unexpected number of the women were Jewish, he was not surprised. He, a Jew active in a Reform temple, suggested that the scholarly tradition combined with the progressive outlook of some branches of Judaism could explain it. How deep the connection between religion and female ambition goes is a question worth probing further.[1] But, whether or not religion was involved, education, plus a willingness to break from traditional roles, was key.

Indeed, it is hard to overstate the importance of education in the lives of these women. Apart from Dahlov Ipcar, whose career as an artist did not require a degree, all went to college, and most had graduate degrees, credentials for their jobs. Some were fortunate to attend excellent high schools. The Wadleigh School, Hunter College High School, Cleveland Heights High School, and Mount Saint Dominic Academy were instrumental in their students' adolescent development. Outside the classroom, many were lucky to have access to cultural experiences, sometimes at home, sometimes in a big city.

Another area of overlap in my mental Venn diagram is the role of fathers. While not every woman had the benefit of a strong relationship with her father, those who did received understanding, encouragement, and sometimes a push—terribly important ingredients for a girl trying to find a place for herself.

Mothers also were pivotal. In some cases, a mother's work outside the home gave her daughter a road map for having both a job and a family. Inside the home, mothers were the organizational glue that kept things running so the rest of the family could go about their lives. Even if a mother did not have a career that her daughter wanted to emulate, she passed on qualities, such as perseverance, optimism, and independence, that her daughter incorporated into her own life.

What else? Every woman in the book was the oldest daughter. The subject of birth order's influence on career and personality is fascinating. The research is still evolving, but it appears that oldest children typically develop certain habits and that parents are highly involved with their oldest, giving rise to ambitious women.[2]

I also note the importance of childcare. Five women were mothers, and four had long-term arrangements with other women who cared for the children when the mothers were working. Dahlov Ipcar was the exception. She worked from her studio at home, and her husband also worked from home, not at an office as the other husbands did. Without others' help, these women could not have achieved what they did.

Then there is the effect of opportunities served up by history. The women in this book saw opportunities rise and fall with events like the Great Depression, the Second World War, and the postwar rush toward domestic stability. In the 1960s, the confluence of the civil rights movement and the second feminist wave benefited women, with effects that lasted decades.

> *Where does it live, that place of permission that lets a person chart a new terrain of possibility, that makes her dare to believe she can be something other than what her culture tells her she is, and then become what she believes she can?*

Maria Popova asks this question in her book *Figuring*. With it, I think she gets to the heart of a woman's ambition. For a very long time, women were cast in roles presumed to be preordained by their inherent feminine qualities. But even when a woman knows she is more complicated than that and can fill multiple roles, she must find a vision for herself and the confidence to realize it. How a woman finds that is what I wanted to know, beginning when I was a young girl, idling away a Sunday afternoon.

Notes

Introduction

1. Seeing feminism only as waves results in an incomplete understanding of history. Women had a variety of experiences outside this framework. Nevertheless, passage of the Nineteenth Amendment in 1920 and the surge of women into professional jobs fifty years later were notable events that mark the ebb and flow of opportunities for many women.

2. "Talk of Feminism Stirs Great Crowd," *New York Times,* February 18, 1914, 2.

3. "Women Suffrage and the Feminist Movement," pamphlet issued by Nebraska Association Opposed to Woman Suffrage, 2, https://history.nebraska.gov/sites/history.nebraska.gov/files/doc/publications/Woman_Suffrage_Feminist.pdf. Fola La Follette was the daughter of Robert M. La Follette Sr., Wisconsin governor, U.S. senator, and founder of the Progressive Party.

4. Government publications provide a trove of information. Particularly helpful were "120 Years of American Education: A Statistical Portrait," U.S. Department of Education, Center for Education Statistics, 69–71, including Fig. 18, https://nces.ed.gov

/pubs93/93442.pdf, and "Women's Occupations through Seven Decades," Women's Bureau Bulletin No. 218 (Washington, D.C.: U.S. Department of Labor, 1947), https://fraser.stlouisfed.org/files/docs /publications/women/b0218_dolwb_1947.pdf.

5. Nancy Cott, *The Grounding of Modern Feminism* (New Haven, Conn.: Yale University Press, 1987), 220. Cott provides detailed analysis of the numbers and cautions that generalizations can mislead, yet the point remains: women's progress in professional fields came to a halt between the first and second waves of feminism.

6. In current parlance of the U.S. Census Bureau, the term *professional* refers to a job that requires a high degree of expertise and training. See http://www.census.gov/glossary. I am more narrowly focused on fields where, in addition to requirements of expertise and training, men were dominant.

7. By 1940, women were numerous in the teaching and nursing fields and far outnumbered men as secretaries and domestics. "Women's Occupations through Seven Decades," 25, 27.

8. Annual conference of Biographers International Organization, Boston, May 26, 2017.

Chapter 1

1. David Fiske, "African American Stage Performer Ella Madison," New York Almanack, https://newyorkalmanack.com/2016/02 /african-american-stage-performer-ella-madison/.

2. "Ella Robinson Madison, Actress and Singer Born," African American Registry, https://aaregistry.org/story/ella-robinson-madison-actress-and-singer-born/.

3. William Zorach, *Art Is My Life* (Cleveland, Ohio: World, 1967), 56.

4. Domestic service, 8 million; clerical, 1.9 million; agricultural, 900,000; teaching, 800,000; clothing manufacture, 575,000; nursing, 288,000; artists, sculptors, and teachers of art, 21,000; physicians, 6,800; lawyers, 3,300. "Women's Occupations through Seven Decades."

5. Lora Heims Tessman, "Fathers and Daughters: Early Tones, Later Echoes," in *Fathers and Their Families,* ed. Stanley H. Cath, Alan Gurwitt, and Linda Gunsberg, 197–223 (Philadelphia: Routledge, 1989).

6. Linda Nochlin, "Why Have There Been No Great Women Artists?," *ArtNews,* January 1971. Nochlin revisited her original essay in

ArtNews, May 30, 2015. Nochlin's question about Picasso's sister echoes Virginia Woolf's about Shakespeare's imaginary sister— would a woman endowed with Shakespeare's talent have been permitted to develop it as he was? Woolf, *A Room of One's Own* (New York: Harcourt Brace, 1929), 50.

7. Jessica Nicoll, "To Be Modern: The Origins of Marguerite and William Zorach's Creative Partnership, 1911–1922," catalog essay in connection with exhibit at Portland Museum of Art, http://www .tfaoi.com/aa/3aa/3aa85.htm.

8. *ArtNews,* March 25, 1933. Excerpt from "'She Was an Original': A Brief History of Women Modernists from New York," *ArtNews,* August 19, 2016, https://www.artnews.com/art-news/retrospective /she-was-an-original-a-brief-history-of-women-modernists-from- new-york-6836/.

9. *O'Keefe, Stettheimer, Torr, Zorach: Women Modernists in New York* was a traveling exhibition that originated at the Norton Museum of Art in West Palm Beach, Florida. I saw it at the Portland Museum of Art.

10. Nancy J. Scott, *Georgia O'Keefe* (London: Reaktion Books, 2015), 87.

11. Marguerite Zorach, "Women in Art," *Christian Science Monitor,* April 12, 1926.

12. Museum of Modern Art, press release, undated, https://www .moma.org/documents/moma_press-release_325144.pdf.

13. Zorach, *Art Is My Life,* 180.

14. Randy Olson, "144 Years of Marriage and Divorce in 1 Chart," http://www.randalolson.com/2015/06/15/144-years-of-marriage -and-divorce-in-1-chart/.

15. Carl Little, *The Art of Dahlov Ipcar* (Camden, Maine: Down East Books, 2010), 41. "Marriage bars," as they were known, existed before the 1930s but became more prevalent during the Depression in an attempt to ration jobs in what was called a "fair" manner. Claudia Goldin, "The Role of World War II in the Rise of Women's Work," NBER Working Paper 3202 (December 1989), 2, https://www .nber.org/papers/w3203.

Chapter 2

1. Muriel preferred the term *Black,* rather than *African American,* because it is more inclusive of the entire African diaspora. I generally use her terminology.

2. Jervis Anderson, *This Was Harlem: A Cultural History, 1900–1950* (New York: Farrar, Straus, and Giroux, 1981).

3. Anderson, 137.

4. Eslanda Goode Robeson, *Paul Robeson: Negro,* quoted in Anderson, 117.

5. Gilbert Osofsky, "A Decade of Urban Tragedy: How Harlem Became a Slum," *New York History* 46, no. 4 (1965): 330–355.

6. Sterling M. Lloyd Jr., "Mission, Vision and Core Values: A Short History," Howard University College of Medicine, May 2006, https://medicine.howard.edu/about-us/mission-vision-and-core-values/short-history. Also, the standards implemented in the wake of the 1910 Flexner Report resulted in the closure of a number of medical schools that had opened to train Black and female students.

7. U.S. Department of Education, Office of Civil Rights, https://www2.ed.gov/about/offices/list/ocr/docs/hq9511.html.

8. National Museum of African American History and Culture, "5 Things to Know: HBCU Edition," https://nmaahc.si.edu/blog-post/5-things-know-hbcu-edition.

9. Ta-Nehisi Coates, *Between the World and Me* (New York: Spiegel and Grau, 2015).

10. Irma Watkins-Owens, *Blood Relations: Caribbean Immigrants and the Harlem Community, 1900–1930* (Bloomington: Indiana University Press, 1996), 50.

11. Saint Augustine, like several schools mentioned in this chapter, is now a university. I refer to it and the other schools by their names at the time.

12. My conversations with Muriel and with her son Charles Woolfolk gave me invaluable insight into Charles Petioni. I also relied on several published sources: Jamie J. Wilson, *Building a Healthy Black Harlem: Health Politics in Harlem, New York, from the Jazz Age to the Great Depression* (Amherst, N.Y.: Cambria Press, 2009); Anthony Appiah and Henry Louis Gates, eds., *Africana: The Encyclopedia of the African and African American Experience* (New York: Civitas Books, 1999); and William Edward Burghardt Du Bois,

The Correspondence of W. E. B. Du Bois, vol. 3 (Amherst: University of Massachusetts Press, 1997).

13. Sarah L. Delany and A. Elizabeth Delany, with Amy Hill Hearth, *Having Our Say: The Delany Sisters' First 100 Years* (New York: Dell, 1994). The 1999 film of the same name (dir. Lynne Littman) starred Diahann Carroll and Ruby Dee.

14. "Modern Ideas Followed in Building New High School," *New York Times,* March 1, 1903.

15. "Shall We Have a Girls' Free Academy?," *New York Times,* December 3, 1855.

16. Mary Roth Walsh, *Doctors Wanted: No Women Need Apply* (Binghamton, N.Y.: Vail-Ballou Press, 1977), 245.

17. Walsh, 186, 194, 224, 230.

18. "History of Harlem Hospital Center," Columbia University Medical Center, http://www.cumc.columbia.edu/harlemhospital /surgery-residency/generalsurgerydept/History%20of%20Harlem %20Hospital%20Center; "Desegregating Harlem Hospital: A Centennial," New York Academy of Medicine, https://nyamcenterforhistory.org/2019/08/26/desegregating-harlem-hospital-a-centennial/.

19. One source suggests that Muriel's father was wary that hiring decisions would be perceived as political and therefore more ambivalent about the assurance that intern slots would go to Black doctors. Wilson, *Building a Healthy Black Harlem,* 78–79.

20. *Montgomery Advertiser,* December 12, 1941. Also helpful were Wesley Phillips Newton's *Montgomery in the Good War: Portrait of a Southern City 1939–1946* (Tuscaloosa: University of Alabama Press, 2000); "149 Years of Leadership," Alabama State University, https:// www.alasu.edu/about-asu/historytradition/149-years-leadership. In 2019, I visited Montgomery's Legacy Museum and National Memorial for Peace and Justice where artifacts are preserved, including the text of laws and regulations cited here.

21. In the middle of the twentieth century, house calls accounted for 40 percent of all physician–patient encounters. By 1980, they accounted for only 1 percent. Leff and Burton, "The Future History of Home Care and Physician House Calls in the United States," *Journals of Gerontology, Series A* 56, no. 10 (2001): M603–8.

22. Anderson, *This Was Harlem,* 347.

23. "History," National Medical Association, https://www.nmanet
.org/page/History. The AMA's past membership policies paralleled
the 1896 Supreme Court decision in *Plessy v. Ferguson* where the
court held that local discriminatory practices did not violate the
federal constitution. Citing "the right of self-governance" of its
constituent groups, the AMA looked the other way when local
groups denied membership to Black doctors. "African American
Physicians and Organized Medicine, 1846–1968," American Medical
Association. https://www.ama-assn.org/sites/ama-assn.org/files
/corp/media-browser/public/ama-history/african-american-
physicians-organized-medicine-timeline.pdf. In 2008, the AMA
apologized for its history of discrimination: https://www.ama-
assn.org/about/ama-history/history-african-americans-and-
organized-medicine.

24. "The Color Line Belts the World," in *W. E. B. Du Bois: A Reader,* ed.
David Levering Lewis (New York: Henry Holt, 1995), 42.

Chapter 3

1. "Eleanor Roosevelt on Pearl Harbor," American Public Media,
https://www.apmreports.org/episode/2014/11/04/eleanor-
roosevelt-on-pearl-harbor.

2. David Brinkley, *Washington Goes to War: The Extraordinary Story of
the Transformation of a City and a Nation* (New York: Knopf, 1988).

3. Information about the early days of OSS comes primarily from
two sources, "The Office of Strategic Services: America's First
Intelligence Agency," Central Intelligence Agency, https://www.cia
.gov/static/7851e16f9e100b6f9cc4ef002028ce2f/Office-of-Strategic-
Services.pdf, and Douglas Waller, *Wild Bill Donovan: The Spymaster
Who Created the OSS and Modern American Espionage* (New York: Free
Press, 2011), 79.

4. Richard Helms and William Hood, *A Look Over My Shoulder: A Life
in the Central Intelligence Agency* (New York: Random House, 2003),
37, 147.

5. Elizabeth P. McIntosh, *Sisterhood of Spies: The Women of the OSS*
(Annapolis, Md.: Naval Institute Press, 1998), 97.

6. Howard McGaw Smyth, "The Ciano Papers: Rose Garden," Central
Intelligence Agency, September 22, 1993, https://www.cia.gov
/library/center-for-the-study-of-intelligence/kent-csi/vol13no2
/html/v13i2a16p_0001.htm#122-covering-memo-by.

7. "The Office of Strategic Services: America's First Intelligence Agency," Central Intelligence Agency, https://www.cia.gov/static /7851e16f9e100b6f9cc4ef002028ce2f/Office-of-Strategic-Services .pdf, and Allen Dulles, *The Secret Surrender* (New York: Harper and Row, 1966).

8. Radomir V. Luza, *The Resistance in Austria, 1938–1945* (Minneapolis: University of Minnesota Press, 1984), 210–214.

9. Nam emigrated to the United States with a visa arranged for by Cordelia and Paul Blum. She settled in New York City where she designed elegant perfume bottles and sold custom-blended fragrances. See Agnes Ash, "Custom Perfume Is Taking Cover in Exotic Wraps," *New York Times,* June 3, 1958. "I was very fond of Nam," Cordelia told me. "A lot of people couldn't quite take her. She was very much Berlin of the twenties, very much like the film *Cabaret*. If people got uptight about morals, they wouldn't have approved of Nam." She shrugged off Nam's affair with the German officer. "That's the age-old story of getting intelligence one way or the other."

10. At the end of Helms's career, Bill Hood helped him write his memoir *A Look over My Shoulder.*

11. In his book, author Tom Mangold describes an internal investigation that Cordelia worked on, late in her career. She was, Mangold writes, "held in great respect within the agency." Mangold, *Cold Warrior: James Jesus Angleton—The CIA's Master Spy Hunter* (New York: Simon and Schuster, 1991), 332.

12. "Percentage of Male and Female by Grade Group, 1951–1957," Central Intelligence Agency, C05866486, September 12, 2013. Job levels were ranked according to the General Schedule. In GS levels 13–15, men were 97 percent. Women were scarce, except in GS levels 1–6.

13. Classified ads, *Boston Daily Globe,* February 8, 1944, 18.

14. Information about women in graduate school and the labor force comes from several sources: Walsh, *Doctors Wanted,* 231; Susan M. Hartmann, *The Home Front and Beyond: American Women in the 1940s* (Boston: Twayne, 1982), 21; Cynthia Grant Bowman, "Women in the Legal Profession from the 1920s to the 1970s: What Can We Learn from Their Experience about Law and Social Change," *Maine Law Review* 61 (2017): 6–8.

15. Katharine Graham, *Personal History* (New York: Alfred A. Knopf, 1977), 416.

16. Adlai Stevenson, "Women in a Free Society," *Smith Alumnae Quarterly,* Summer 1955, 195–97, https://saqonline.smith.edu /publication/?m=45764&i=431244&p=10.

Chapter 4

1. Martha Lipson Lepow, MD, interview by Danielle Wales, MD, PhD, American Academy of Pediatrics, Oral History Project, January 11 and 30, March 6, 2017, https://www.aap.org/en-us /Documents/Lepow_interview.pdf.

2. "Dr. John Lyon Caughey, Jr.," in *Encyclopedia of Cleveland History,* Case Western Reserve University, http://ech.case.edu/ech-cgi /article.pl?id=CDJLJ.

3. Walsh, *Doctors Wanted,* 245, Table 9, 268–69, Table 10.

4. Martha Lipson Lepow, MD, interview.

5. Martha Lepow, "Love in the Virus Lab," in *Polio,* ed. Thomas M. Daniel and Frederick C. Robbins (Rochester, N.Y.: University of Rochester Press, 1997), 137.

6. "Polio Elimination in the United States," Centers for Disease Control and Prevention, https://www.cdc.gov/polio/what-is-polio /polio-us.html.

7. Sophie Ochmann, "Polio," 2017, https://ourworldindata.org/polio.

8. For an overview of the development of pediatric medicine, see Perri Klass, *A Good Time to Be Born: How Science and Public Health Gave Children a Future* (New York: W. W. Norton, 2020).

9. Lepow, "Love in the Virus Lab," 141.

10. Eli Ginzberg and Alice M. Yohalem, *Educated American Women: Self-Portraits* (New York: Columbia University Press, 1966). The study was conducted on women enrolled in graduate programs at Columbia during the six years after World War II, a relevant time period for the women in this book.

11. Lisa Grunwald and Stephen J. Adler, eds., *Letters of the Century, America 1900–1999* (New York: Dial Press, 1999), 395.

12. Lepow, "Love in the Virus Lab," 155.

13. Lepow, 155.

14. U.S. Department of Labor, *1960 Handbook on Women Workers,* Women's Bureau Bulletin 275 (Washington, D.C.: U.S. Department

of Labor, 1960), 8, 10, https://babel.hathitrust.org/cgi/pt?id=osu
.32435026126581.

15. Cathleen F. Crowley, "At 80, Doctor Not Yet Ready to Stop
Working," *Times Union,* April 12, 2007.

Chapter 5

1. "NASA's Origins and the Dawn of the Space Age," a monograph
published by NASA, discusses the psychological effect of Sputnik on
the American populace; see https://history.nasa.gov/monograph10
/onesmlbl.htm.

2. Hope Jahrens, *Lab Girl* (New York: Vintage, 2017).

3. "Size of the Nanoscale," National Nanotechnology Initiative,
https://www.nano.gov/nanotech-101/what/nano-size. Also important in the development of nanotechnology was the discovery of
nanoparticles and quantum dots. For an explanation of Millie's
work in her own words, I found several sources helpful, including
Mildred S. Dresselhaus, "Reflections on My Career in Condensed
Matter Physics," *Annual Review of Condensed Matter Physics* 2 (2011):
1–9.

4. Though low, women's share of doctorates in 1958 was about half
what it was in 1945. "120 Years of American Education: A Statistical
Portrait," 83, Table 28.

5. Eleanor Roosevelt mentioned Greenwich House in her syndicated
newspaper column. See *My Day,* July 2, 1943, https://www2.gwu
.edu/~erpapers/myday/browsebyyear.cfm.

6. Leonard Bernstein, as told to his brother Burton Bernstein, "The
Debut Concert," Leonard Bernstein Office, https://leonardbernstein
.com/about/conductor/historic-concerts/the-debut-concert-1943.

7. "Young Aide Leads Philharmonic, Steps in When Bruno Walter Is
Ill," *New York Times,* November 15, 1943, 1.

8. https://library.hunter.cuny.edu/sites/default/files/documents
/archives/finding_aids/Normal_College_Collection_Finding_Aid
.pdf.

9. David McCullough recollected Kahn's quote in his interview with
the *Paris Review* in *Art of Biography* 2, no. 152 (1999).

10. "Rosalyn Yalow: Biographical," http://www.nobelprize.org
/nobel_prizes/medicine/laureates/1977/yalow-bio.html.

11. I am indebted to several sources for some of this biographical
information, particularly Magdolna Hargittai and Istvan Hargittai,

Candid Science IV: Conversations with Famous Physicists (London: Imperial College Press, 2004), 550, 557, and "Carbon Catalyst for Half a Century: A Conversation with Mildred Dresselhaus," *New York Times,* July 3, 2012, https://www.nytimes.com/2012/07/03/science/carbon-catalyst-for-half-a-century.html.

12. MIT Policies and Procedures, Sec. 2.2.1 lays out the exceedingly high criteria for Institute Professor: https://policies.mit.edu/policies-procedures/20-faculty-and-other-academic-appointments/22-special-professorial-appointments.

13. After Millie's death in 2017, MIT and other institutions hosted tributes to her, and I am indebted to the many published comments. This story from Marianne Cooper was published as "My Extended Family: Growing Up as the Daughter of Millie Dresselhaus," *Celebrating Millie,* May 15, 2018, https://millie.pubpub.org/pub/6c8d1jyi.

14. "Leora Cooper on the Legacy of Her Grandmother, Mildred Dresselhaus," *MIT News,* http://news.mit.edu/2017/3q-leora-cooper-legacy-of-her-grandmother-mildred-dresselhaus-0227.

Chapter 6

1. The mosaic murals are the work of artist Lisa Houck; see https://www.lisahouck.com/public-art.

2. Recent articles document similar practices in a number of cultures. "'Virginity Test' Still Haunts Some Indian Brides," *Asia Times,* March 13, 2019, https://asiatimes.com/2019/03/virginity-test-still-haunts-some-indian-brides/; "Virginity or Death for Afghan Brides," *Radio Free Europe,* December 6, 2015, https://www.rferl.org/a/afghanistan-virgin-brides-punishment/27409971.html; "Jewish Brides, Premarital Sex, and Patriarchal Ownership of Female Bodies," *Tablet Magazine,* February 10, 2015, https://www.tabletmag.com/sections/belief/articles/daf-yomi-115-kirsch.

3. *Teen Time* was one of many magazines aimed at teenagers that sprang up in the 1950s and early 1960s. One journalism professor at the time considered such magazines as both confessional, with teen girls asking for advice on relationships with boys, and cultish, with features on handsome rock-and-roll stars and the like. *Teen Time* carried such content, plus fan club news, but also distinguished itself by including an article on the Peace Corps in its inaugural issue. For future issues, its adult editors and panel of teen advisors

planned content such as political forums and book reviews. Charles H. Brown, "Self-Portrait: The Teen-Type Magazine," *Annals of the American Academy of Political and Social Science* 338 (November 1961): 13–21, https://www-jstor-org.ezproxy.bpl.org/stable/1034662?seq =1#metadata_info_tab_contents.

4. Caroline Framke, "10 Years Ago, *Mad Men* Began a Story of Men Who Tried to Change—and the Women Who Actually Did," *Vox,* July 19, 2017, https://www.vox.com/culture/2017/7/19/15992342 /mad-men-anniversary-don-peggy-joan.

5. "Shun Conformity, Warren Advises," *New York Times,* June 3, 1964, https://timesmachine.nytimes.com/timesmachine/1964/06/03 /106975622.pdf.

6. For an understanding of this period of Boston's history, particularly its racial and ethnic dimensions, I am indebted to the dissertation of Tatiana Maria Fernandez Cruz, based in part on interviews with Frieda Garcia and Hubie Jones, "Boston's Struggle in Black and Brown: Racial Politics, Community Development, and Grassroots Organizing 1960–1985," https://deepblue.lib.umich.edu/bitstream /handle/2027.42/140982/tatianac_1.pdf.

7. https://academicarchive.snhu.edu/bitstream/handle/10474/2587 /Henry_Steele_Commager_06_03_1974.pdf.

8. U.S. President's Commission on the Status of Women Records, Collection Overview, John F. Kennedy Library and Museum, https://www.jfklibrary.org/asset-viewer/archives/USPCSW.

9. Jim Tankersley, *The Riches of This Land* (New York: Public Affairs, 2020), 87.

10. *9to5: The Story of a Movement,* an independent film, documents the group's beginning and growth; see https://itvs.org/films/9to5.

11. Culbreath v. Dukakis, 695 F. Supp. 1350 (D. Mass. 1988).

12. George Schlichte, *Politics in the Purple Kingdom: The Derailment of Vatican II* (New York: Sheed and Ward, 1993).

13. The sculptors are Fern Cunningham and Meta Vaux Warwick Fuller.

Chapter 7

1. Virginia Woolf, "I Am Christina Rossetti," in *The Second Common Reader* (San Diego, Calif.: Harcourt, 1986).

2. Myra Bradwell had already obtained an exemption from the state legislature that allowed her, as a married woman, to publish a

newspaper and keep her earnings; see https://www.supremecourt
.gov/visiting/exhibitions/LadyLawyers/section1.aspx.

3. Bradwell v. Illinois, 84 U.S. (16 *Wall.*) 130, 141 (1873). Because each
state sets its own licensing requirements, women faced differing
restrictions.

4. In re Goodell, 39 Wis. 232 (1875). Four years later, the legislature
passed a measure authorizing bar admission for female practitioners; 48 Wis. 693 (1879).

5. Joyce Antler, *The Educated Woman and Professionalization: The
Struggle for a New Feminine Identity, 1890–1920* (New York: Garland,
1987), 269–70.

6. Census data from 1920 show a total of 150,007 physicians,
surgeons, and osteopaths, 8,892 of them women, just under 6
percent. Also 122,519 lawyers, judges, and justices, 1,738 of them
women, or about 1 percent. "Comparative Occupation Statistics,
1870–1940," 111 and 128, Tables 8 and 10, https://www2.census
.gov/library/publications/decennial/1940/population-occupation
/00312147ch2.pdf.

7. Kaiser Family Foundation, "Professionally Active Physicians by
Gender," March 2020, https://www.kff.org/other/state-indicator
/physicians-by-gender/?currentTimeframe=0&sortModel=
%7B%22colId%22:%22Location%22,%22sort%22:%22asc%22%7D, and
American Bar Association, National Lawyer Population Survey,
2020, https://www.americanbar.org/content/dam/aba
/administrative/market_research/national-lawyer-population-
demographics-2010–2020.pdf. Although race is not my focus, it
bears repeating that only a small percentage of doctors and lawyers
identify themselves as Black, Asian, or Hispanic.

8. Jeannie Suk Gersen, "The Socratic Method in the Age of Trauma,"
Harvard Law Review 130 (2017): 2320–47.

9. Paul Massari, "HLS Fetes 50 Years of Women Graduates," *Harvard
Gazette,* May 8, 2003, https://news.harvard.edu/gazette/story/2003
/05/hls-fetes-50-years-of-women-graduates/.

10. Bowman, "Women in the Legal Profession," 7–8.

11. William E. Stacy, U.S. Army Border Operations in Germany,
1945–83, U.S. Army Center of Military History, 1984, https://history
.army.mil/documents/BorderOps/ch1.htm.

12. Tony Judt, *Postwar: A History of Europe since 1945* (New York:
Penguin, 2005), 87.

13. In December 1946, President Truman had ordered the ship, which had once carried military cargo under a different name, across the Atlantic to begin retrieving displaced persons. "Statement by the President Concerning the Transportation of Refugees to the United States," December 19, 1946, https://www.presidency.ucsb.edu/documents/statement-the-president-concerning-the-transportation-refugees-the-united-states.

14. Ruth Bader Ginsburg began studying law at Harvard in 1956, the year Rya Zobel graduated.

15. "Goodwin Procter, 100 Years, 1912–2012," 50, https://www.goodwinlaw.com/-/media/files/our-firm/centennial_book.pdf.

16. Mark Joseph Stern, "Carter's Quiet Revolution," *Slate,* July 14, 2019, https://slate.com/news-and-politics/2019/07/jimmy-carter-diversity-judges-donald-trump-court-nominees.html.

17. The other three female candidates included two state court judges and a lawyer who later served on the state appeals court. "14 Finalists for New US Judgeships," *Boston Globe,* November 14, 1978, 24.

18. In 1860, two African American men sat on a Massachusetts jury, ninety years before any woman; see https://www.mass.gov/info-details/learn-about-the-history-of-the-jury-system#expanding-the-concept-of-%22juror%22-.

19. Kai Bird, *The Outlier: The Unfinished Presidency of Jimmy Carter* (New York: Crown, 2021), 207.

20. "There Go the Judges," *Boston Globe,* July 9, 1994.

21. The selection committee for the Devitt Award is chaired by a justice of the U.S. Supreme Court, in this case Neil Gorsuch. District of Massachusetts public announcement, September 29, 2020, https://www.mad.uscourts.gov/general/pdf/announce/Judge%20Zobel%20Edward%20J.%20Devitt%20Distinguished%20Service%20to%20Justice%20Award.pdf.

22. " Judge Rya Zobel to Receive 2020 Devitt Award," *U.S. Courts News,* October 20, 2020, https://www.uscourts.gov/news/2020/10/20/judge-rya-zobel-receive-2020-devitt-award.

Epilogue

1. Historian Joyce Antler has written about this issue in *The Journey Home: How Jewish Women Shaped Modern America* (New York: Schocken Books, 1998) and *Jewish Radical Feminism: Voices from the*

Women's Liberation Movement (New York: New York University Press, 2018).

2. Sandra E. Black, "A New Economic Study Shows How Your Birth Order Can Influence Your Career," Brookings Institution, April 19, 2017, https://www.brookings.edu/opinions/a-new-economic-study-shows-how-your-birth-order-can-influence-your-career/.

Further Reading

For Memoir and Group Biography

Barnet, Andrea. *Visionary Women: How Rachel Carson, Jane Jacobs and Alice Waters Changed Our World*. New York: Ecco, 2018.

Dean, Michelle. *Sharp: The Women Who Made an Art of Having an Opinion*. New York: Grove Press, 2018.

Graham, Katharine. *Personal History*. New York: Alfred A. Knopf, 1997.

Holt, Nathalia. *Rise of the Rocket Girls: The Women Who Propelled Us, from Missiles to the Moon to Mars*. New York: Little, Brown, 2016.

Katz, Catherine Grace. *The Daughters of Yalta: The Churchills, Roosevelts, and Harrimans—A Story of Love and War*. Boston: Houghton Mifflin Harcourt, 2020.

Mundy, Liza. *Code Girls: The True Story of the American Women Who Secretly Broke Codes in World War II*. New York: Hachette, 2017.

Napoli, Lisa. *Susan, Linda, Nina, and Cokie. The Extraordinary Story of the Founding Mothers of NPR*. New York: Abrams Press, 2021.

Pollack, Eileen. *The Only Woman in the Room: Why Science Is Still a Boys' Club*. Boston: Beacon Press, 2015.

Robertson, Nan. *The Girls in the Balcony: Women, Men, and the "New York Times."* New York: Random House, 1992.

Shetterly, Margot Lee. *Hidden Figures.* New York: HarperCollins, 2016.

Tubbs, Anna Malaika. *The Three Mothers: How the Mothers of Martin Luther King, Jr., Malcolm X, and James Baldwin Shaped a Nation.* New York: Flatiron Books, 2021.

For Historical and Theoretical Framework

Collins, Patricia Hill. *Black Feminist Thought: Knowledge, Consciousness, and the Politics of Empowerment,* 2nd ed. New York: Routledge, 2000.

Coontz, Stephanie. *A Strange Stirring: The Feminine Mystique and American Women at the Dawn of the 1960s.* New York: Basic Books, 2011.

Cott, Nancy F. *The Grounding of Modern Feminism.* New Haven, Conn.: Yale University Press, 1987.

Crenshaw, Kimberlé. Forthcoming. *On Intersectionality: Selected Writings.* New York: New Press.

Drachman, Virginia. *Sisters in Law: Women Lawyers in Modern American History.* Cambridge, Mass.: Harvard University Press, 1998.

Drachman, Virginia. *Women Lawyers and the Origins of Professional Identity in America: Letters of the Equity Club, 1887–1890.* Ann Arbor: University of Michigan Press, 1993.

Jones, Martha S. *Vanguard: How Black Women Broke Barriers, Won the Vote, and Insisted upon Equality for All.* New York: Basic Books, 2020.

May, Elaine Tyler. *Homeward Bound: American Families in the Cold War Era,* 4th ed. New York: Basic Books, 2017.

Meyerowitz, Joanne. *Not June Cleaver: Women and Gender in Postwar America, 1945–1960.* Philadelphia: Temple University Press, 1994.

Rosenberg, Rosalind. *Beyond Separate Spheres: Intellectual Roots of Feminism.* New Haven, Conn.: Yale University Press, 1982.

Tetrault, Lisa. *The Myth of Seneca Falls: Memory and the Women's Suffrage Movement, 1848–1898.* Chapel Hill: University of North Carolina Press, 2014.

Questions for Discussion

1. What fact surprised you most about the historical period in which the women in the book came of age, the fifty years between 1920 and 1970?
2. What surprised/delighted/frustrated you most about the circumstances the women faced?
3. In the book's epilogue, Kathleen draws conclusions about experiences and influences that fostered the women's ambitions. Do you think additional or different conclusions can be drawn?
4. Are the factors that motivated ambition in older generations of women still important to girls and young women today? If other factors are more important in fostering ambition today, what are they?
5. During the COVID-19 pandemic, many women in the workforce left their jobs or switched jobs. What do you think the short-term future holds for women in professional jobs? What about the longer term?
6. Some of the women in the book talked about the role of socioeconomic class in their lives. For instance, Muriel

Petioni said her middle-class upbringing meant that she, as a doctor, substantially overcame the challenges posed by race and gender. In your life, is socioeconomic class as significant as it was for Dr. Petioni? Is it a positive factor for you?

7. Mildred Dresselhaus also referred to socioeconomic class when she talked about the importance of acquiring "background." Cordelia Hood mentioned "background," too, in the sense that her family had an extensive library, whereas some of their neighbors had none at all. What sort of "background" is required for success in the professional world today? What steps should be taken to ensure that girls and young women have the appropriate background for professional jobs, and who should take them? Is it preferable or possible to dispense with class distinctions?

8. When women achieve success in male-dominated professional fields, does their success help perpetuate male viewpoints and standards of behavior? Are certain standards gender-neutral?

9. In her book *We Should All Be Feminists,* Chimananda Ngozi Adichie gives this definition of a feminist: *a person who believes in the social, political, and economic equality of the sexes.* Is it important to have a definition? Do you agree with this definition? Do you want to suggest any modifications?

Index

Page numbers in italics refer to photographs and other illustrations.

CPSIA information can be obtained
at www.ICGtesting.com
Printed in the USA
LVHW091815110222
710916LV00020B/457/J